D1527624

Critical Perspectives on Service-Learning in Higher Education

Critical Perspectives on Service-Learning in Higher Education

Susan J. Deeley
University of Glasgow, UK

First published 2015 by
PALGRAVE MACMILLAN

Palgrave Macmillan in the UK is an imprint of Macmillan Publishers Limited,
registered in England, company number 785998, of Houndmills, Basingstoke,
Hampshire RG21 6XS.

Palgrave Macmillan in the US is a division of St Martin's Press LLC,
175 Fifth Avenue, New York, NY 10010.

Palgrave Macmillan is the global academic imprint of the above companies
and has companies and representatives throughout the world.

Palgrave® and Macmillan® are registered trademarks in the United States,
the United Kingdom, Europe and other countries

ISBN: 978–1–137–38324–2

This book is printed on paper suitable for recycling and made from fully
managed and sustained forest sources. Logging, pulping and manufacturing
processes are expected to conform to the environmental regulations of the
country of origin.

A catalogue record for this book is available from the British Library.

A catalog record for this book is available from the Library of Congress.

In loving memory of
Astri and Donald
and
with love to
Kenneth and Hazel

Contents

Acknowledgements

Hearty thanks to my service-learning students who inspired me to write this book and who willingly participated in my research. I am delighted to have the opportunity to present their coursework, albeit anonymously. So, my special thanks to the students in the classes of 2006–7, 2008–9, 2010–11, and 2012–13. My thanks also to Linda Chisholm who very kindly gave her permission for me to use her iconic book, *Charting a Hero's Journey* (2000), without which my book would have been incomplete and my students' reflective tutorials unstructured. I am also very grateful to Linda for her friendship and guidance in my own service-learning journey. Thanks to all the staff and service-users in the community agencies who have generously hosted service-learning placements and without whom my service-learning courses would not be possible. In particular, thanks to Grace Lamont, who has warmly welcomed service-learning students regularly since 1998 and to Phra Saneh Dhammavaro for warmly welcoming me. Also, my thanks to Andrew James, the Commissioning Editor at Palgrave Macmillan, for giving me the opportunity to publish this book; Beth O'Leary and Eleanor Christie for helping me through the publishing processes; the publishing team; the anonymous referee for helpful and constructive feedback on my book proposal; and to my friends and colleagues in the international service-learning community from whom I have learned. Thanks to Robert Yule for his diligence in preparing the cover photograph of my mother's art design. Last, but not least, my thanks to Kenneth Deeley and Hazel Deeley for their love and support as always.

1
Introduction

Background

I first encountered service-learning in 1998 when I was asked to convene a course to international students at a Scottish university. I have taught the course annually ever since. The number of students on my course varied at different times: typically one year there would be perhaps three or four students whereas in another year there would be over twenty students. The course was not offered to home students until 2006, when, as the director of the Public Policy undergraduate programme, I introduced service-learning in the Public Policy curriculum to our honours students, as part of the MA (Social Sciences) undergraduate degree. This arrangement secured service-learning to the mainstream learning and teaching agenda at the university. To embed and support this further, I undertook a research study on the effects of service-learning on students for my dissertation as part of an MEd in Academic Practice, which I was awarded in 2007. Throughout these years of my teaching, I combed the extant service-learning literature in an effort to enhance student learning and to support my teaching. Unfortunately, it became increasingly frustrating as I struggled to find literature that would enable students' further understanding of this innovative pedagogy. I could not find any particularly helpful literature that could be utilised appropriately as the main advanced text in the context of a university service-learning course. I was not searching for an instructional handbook, rather, I was seeking a more theoretical and analytical text that would challenge my students' thinking and critical analysis of their service-learning, while also supporting my teaching. I felt that the dearth of appropriate resources was a disservice to my students and so I was motivated to write this book, which is a result of a culmination of various learning and teaching experiences and research activities.

The book involves the dissemination of recent findings from my empirical research on service-learning, authentic examples from my service-learning students' coursework, examples from my own voluntary work service that I undertook at the same time as my students, and excerpts from my journal while participating in international service-learning in Thailand. Ultimately, my overall aims are to offer a unique and engaging insight to service-learning pedagogy and to begin to fill a gap in the literature with its critical and in-depth analysis of theory and practice in service-learning.

This first chapter presents the overall aims of the book and a brief overview of its content. It then provides a 'navigational route map' and a succinct summary of the contents of each chapter. The book does not necessitate a sequential reading as individual chapters can be extracted separately and used for discussion with students. This means that it can be used easily as a learning and teaching resource. Chapters 2–4 are more theoretically based than the later chapters. By contrast, Chapters 5–7 lean towards a practical approach and are grounded in my students' learning experiences in this field and are informed by the findings from my empirical qualitative research on service-learning. Chapter 8 presents a summary of and a conclusion to the book. It involves a critical evaluation that leads to the identification of areas that are ripe for further research. I finish with some of my own reflections.

Aims

Overall, the book aims to provide an in-depth and critical perspective of service-learning, which is supported by empirical evidence from my practitioner research. One of the objectives of the book is to seek a conceptual framework for service-learning. This is found by asserting a theoretical paradigm which is grounded in extant learning theories. Another essential goal of this book is to venture further in an investigation to the possible function of service-learning, not merely as citizenship education, but as critical pedagogy.

There is a specific focus in the book on critical reflection, academic writing, and assessment in service-learning. Moreover, as the book examines reflective practice, it is also relevant for educational practitioners involved with students undertaking any type of work placement or vocational education. As I have said elsewhere (Deeley, 2014; 2010), service-learning is aptly placed to provide students with opportunities to develop advanced critical thinking skills, competencies, and attributes which are transferable to their future workplace. This is pertinent in a globally competitive workplace, where employers typically expect graduates to have more than subject-specific skills related to their degree (Hinchliffe and Jolly, 2011; Knight, 2006).

The overarching rationale for the book is to provide service-learning students with the opportunity to gain broader knowledge and in-depth understanding of this type of experiential learning and to provide an in-depth theoretical analysis of service-learning, which can serve to inform the academic practice of service-learning teachers.

In order to achieve its aims, the specific objectives of the book are to:

- define and outline service-learning;
- provide a theoretical model for this type of learning;
- explore the potential functions and outcomes of this type of pedagogy;
- examine the practice and effects of critical reflection as part of learning;
- demonstrate examples of academic writing in service-learning through students' coursework and model examples provided from the teacher's experience; and
- evaluate the effects of students' critical reflection within and on assessment in service-learning using empirical evidence from my research.

Summary of the book's content

Service-learning unites theory and practice by drawing together aspects that are mutually informative. The book reflects this design through its underpinning thematic structure of theory (Chapters 2–4) and practice (Chapters 5–7). Beginning with a review of the literature, the book seeks to raise awareness and understanding of student learning by examining the nature of service-learning: what it entails; its purpose; and how it could be utilised in relation to citizenship education. Reaching further back to its roots, an exploration is made to the possible conceptual sources of service-learning by drawing on experiential learning theory. It is then argued that this type of non-traditional learning and teaching dovetails with critical pedagogy. After proposing a theoretical paradigm for service-learning and its possible function as critical pedagogy, the book moves on to examine critical reflection, which plays an essential role within service-learning. Critical reflection, as part of critical thinking, is an essential metacognitive skill for students to connect their practical voluntary work service experiences on placement with the abstract concepts and theoretical dimensions of the coursework. The practical aspects of service-learning are examined in terms of academic writing. Being a non-traditional pedagogy, it is appropriate that it is aligned with non-traditional assessment methods. Authentic examples of students' coursework are used to exemplify such assessment methods as journal writing and the reporting of 'critical incidents'. As a unique point in the text, there are also examples from my own service-learning experiences.

The assessment methods referred to in the book are transferable as reflective practice for use in other types of academic or professional courses. There is a dissemination of empirical findings from my recent research study on service-learning students' reflections in and on unconventional assessment methods. Included in this is an innovative summative co-assessment method used for student oral presentations in their service-learning coursework. Its value to students' future employment through the enhancement of their skills and attributes within service-learning is reported elsewhere (Deeley, 2014). Finally, the book concludes with a summary and analysis of the value of service-learning and its role, as seen through the lens of critical pedagogy.

A 'navigational route map'

Following this introductory first chapter, the aim of Chapter 2 is to place service-learning in context. It begins with an exploration of its meaning using references to a metaphorical nautical journey. In the second chapter, an explanation of how service-learning is constructed as an accredited academic course, with specific reference to its use for undergraduate students in higher education, is given. Although service-learning is multidisciplinary and adaptable across the curriculum, the examples used in this book are applicable primarily to the social and political sciences. Initially, a historical perspective will be taken to discover and explore the essential origins of service-learning in practice. For fuller understanding and appreciation of a 'technical' perspective (Butin, 2010, p. 8) of this pedagogy, its definitions, characteristics, and principles are investigated through an in-depth literature review. Other aspects of service-learning are also examined, such as its role in citizenship education and its compatibility with socio-political activities, in particular concerning social justice. This chapter also includes summary observations from the literature concerning the overarching effects of service-learning and draws on references from my own empirical research in this field. This also connects to the more in-depth discussion of empirical findings from my further service-learning research disseminated later in Chapter 7.

Disappointingly, there is a dearth of evidence from the extant literature that provides in-depth critical analysis of the theoretical, philosophical, and educational sources of service-learning. Chapter 3 modestly attempts to address this gap by exploring theoretical perspectives and searching diverse sources that are compatible with, and offer an appropriate contribution to, a conceptual framework for service-learning. Drawing on the ideas of Dewey, Vygotsky, and Piaget this third chapter explores conceptual and philosophical approaches to the making of meaning and understanding, through experience, language, and thought. As service-learning involves learning through experience various forms of an experiential learning cycle can be used effectively in structuring students' critical reflections. Experiential learning theory thus provides a major contribution to a theoretical paradigm for this pedagogy. Adult learning theories, including Mezirow's transformative theory, are also pertinent to a theoretical paradigm for service-learning in higher education. In addition, the ideas of Rogers, Shor, and Freire provide a further dimension to a theoretical paradigm because they are analogous with the facilitation of collaborative and active learning in a democratic classroom. Although service-learning can take diverse forms, it consists of key components that can be effectively grounded in various extant theories. Service-learning is, therefore, the sum of its parts. Weaving the various threads or parts together with associated theories and influential ideas of significant individuals such as Dewey and Freire, for example, provides a theoretical paradigm for service-learning. Additionally, it is asserted that critical theory may also contribute an important strand to this paradigm, shifting service-learning into the realm of critical pedagogy. This contributes to an emerging complex pattern for service-learning and is the focus of the next chapter.

Chapter 4 provides an argument for service-learning as a critical pedagogy. With reference to critical theory and Freirean pedagogy, the role of service-learning in education as a social and political process is investigated. There is an exploration of the process of conscientisation and students' raised awareness because these factors are inextricably linked as potential consequences of critical reflection in service-learning. Conscientisation, or raised consciousness, is examined with reference to examples from the writings of Freire and Malcolm X. Further reference is made to Mezirow's transformative theory, which involves the effects and implications of change to students' meaning schemes and meaning perspectives. The basis for change originates in, and emerges from, the exercise of students' critical reflection.

Critical reflection, as a form of critical thinking and an essential component of service-learning, is closely analysed in Chapter 5. It follows on from the ideas presented in the preceding chapter on the concept of conscientisation and critical pedagogy. Questions concerning how and why critical reflection can be used are addressed. The facilitation of critical reflection is also a feature of this fifth chapter, in particular the use of critical incidents, which are then further explored in Chapter 6 on academic writing in service-learning. It is asserted that critical reflection, which connects theory with practice, can deepen student's learning, raise their awareness of social and political issues, and have the potential of motivating students to engage in praxis, or informed critical action for social justice.

Chapter 6 focuses on academic writing in service-learning. This is typically different from traditional academic writing because of the personal and affective elements that are involved in experiential learning. Being more appropriate genres, reflective writing and the use of the narrative are examined. Reflective writing is an integral part of service-learning and serves two purposes. Firstly, reflective writing is used as a means of facilitating critical reflection and learning. For both formative and summative assessment in my service-learning courses, students are required to write 'critical incident' reports. Sample models of these reports written from my own experience are analysed by my students in class in order to help their understanding of this critical reflective and writing process. I use examples from my international service and from my service in the United Kingdom that I undertook at the same time as my students. To safeguard anonymity of service-users, however, only the international example is presented in this chapter. An interesting example from a student's 'critical incident' report is also presented in this chapter.

Secondly, reflective writing is used for assessment as an academic requirement for accreditation. Students are not assessed for their voluntary work in the community per se. Instead, they are assessed for the written assignment resulting from their critical reflection on their service in the community and the connections they make with conceptual ideas within the academic coursework. Reflective journal writing is a process and results in an end product. In this respect, students may keep a 'working' journal or diary, and then submit a 'formal' journal to be summatively assessed. An excerpt from my own reflective service-learning journal is presented as a sample model. The excerpt is one that I use with my own students and is from my international service in Thailand. In addition, examples from students' journals are also presented to demonstrate the connections students have made between their service and the academic coursework.

Following on from the previous chapter, Chapter 7 presents empirical evidence from my practitioner research involving students' reflections in and on assessment used in service-learning. The assessment methods are outlined and explained, with particular attention to innovative summative co-assessment methods (Deeley, 2014), which are transferable to other academic courses and may contribute, not only to the enhancement of students' employability skills, competencies and graduate attributes, but to deep and life-long learning.

Chapter 8, as the final chapter, brings the ideas and critical perspectives that have been presented in the book together in the form of a summary. From this aspect, a critical evaluation follows, which argues that the value of service-learning for students lies in the opportunities it offers them to develop criticality. Criticality is not merely critical thinking, but also subsequent critical action, which, ultimately and ideally, leads to lifelong critical development.

From a critical perspective, it is important that the potential short-comings, misunderstandings, and disadvantages of service-learning are not overlooked or minimised. Nevertheless, in the light of my research, teaching experience, positive and enduring relationships with my students, service-learning is undoubtedly, for me, the 'crème de la crème' (Spark, 1965, p. 14). Emerging from the critical evaluation in this chapter, areas in service-learning for further research and analysis are identified. Finally, this particular investigative journey ends with some reflections.

2
Contextualising Service-Learning

Introduction

The aim of this chapter is to present an overview of service-learning in the context of higher education. Essentially, service-learning combines service to the community with academic study. These two aspects of service and study are interrelated: students study an academic course in a field that is connected with their service in the community. Typically, academic credit is awarded for assignments related to the academic study and informed by the student's community service experience. The learning gained from the latter is usually assessed through a reflective journal, although the service per se is not assessed. 'Service-learning' is a generic term used in education and does not belong to any particular academic discipline. Indeed, one of its strengths is that it can be utilised in different ways in a range of disciplinary contexts. Although service-learning is multidisciplinary, it nestles comfortably within the public policy domain of citizenship education, from which the examples of service-learning in the book are drawn.

It is of value to establish an understanding of service-learning at this early stage of the book because service-learning is not widespread in the United Kingdom, and its use in the context of higher education is fairly uncommon. The main source of the service-learning movement and its literature hails from North America, which is not surprising because there it is more culturally and educationally embedded. Nonetheless, service-learning is becoming a global educational phenomenon, and its links to the concepts of social justice, citizenship, and community play an important role in the development of critical thinking graduates.

In this chapter, historical perspectives will be taken first of all and with reference to two particular concepts closely connected with service-learning. One of these concepts is voluntarism and its impact both in the United States and in the United Kingdom. The second concept is that of citizenship, which is seen in terms of education policy. Following this, the meaning of service-learning and what it entails will be explored. Service-learning can be perceived as a journey, but the route to its meaning is another type of journey. Trawling through the literature for an agreed definition of 'service-learning' is an onerous task. Indeed, Stanton (1990a, p. 65) affirms this, commenting that '[f]inding a single, firm, universally acceptable definition of service learning is like navigating through fog'. Continuing the nautical analogy, it would be fair to say that several crows appear in sight overhead to direct the way to some understanding of service-learning. En route are various promontories where docking is possible. The landscape from a vantage point afforded by Furco (2003) consists of over two hundred definitions, diverse characteristics, and a number of sets of principles. Nevertheless, disembarking at any one of these promontories would not suffice because an adequate cargo of knowledge of service-learning would not, at this stage, have been acquired. It is necessary to sail on through a plethora of literature which provides further insight into the nature of service-learning. Most of this literature, however, is in the form of quantitative research studies, which attempt to measure and depict the journey of service-learning as invariably having beneficial effects on students. Unfortunately, there is a dearth of critical analysis of how and why these effects actually occur. Furthermore, little is reported of any potential maelstroms or negative aspects of service-learning. The studies by Jones (2002), Jones et al. (2005), and Deeley (2007) are a few exceptions to this, as they explore the darker waters of service-learning. Other aspects of service-learning concern the effects of students' service on the community and on teachers. The former has been investigated to some extent (Deeley, 2004), but it remains a largely unexplored territory. The effects of service-learning on teachers are also much of an uncharted area of research. In sum, the major trends in the literature focus on the benefits of service-learning to students, which only partially, and by implication, provides an understanding of this pedagogy.

The body of research reveals that there remains much to be discovered about service-learning, such as the nature of its educational theory and thus its pedagogical effectiveness. Much of the extant service-learning research concerns quantitative studies that attempt to measure the efficacy of service-learning. This is based on an assumption that a positivist approach is appropriate. Service-learning is about learning and teaching, about people in widely diverse circumstances, and about sometimes unforeseen and unpredictable experiences. Bearing these factors in mind, qualitative research might offer richer opportunities to capture more effectively the outcomes of service-learning, as concurred by Butin (2010, p. 38), who says that 'service-learning is analogous to teaching and other "wickedly" complex problems defying quantitative solutions'.

It is generally claimed and accepted that service-learning originates from the philosophical and educational theoretical writings of John Dewey (1916; 1938) predominantly, and also of David Kolb (1984). Disappointingly, it is evident that much of the literature on service-learning uses similar citations regarding its theoretical grounding with little evidence of further in-depth or diverse enquiry. Critics of service-learning may be justified in their scepticism if faced with a desert of critical evaluation and empirical evidence to support claims of its efficacy. Contextualising service-learning from a theoretical and critical perspective provides a much needed oasis and fills a gap in the relevant literature (Butin, 2010). As the overall aim of the book is to provide a comprehensive and critical understanding of service-learning in higher education, it is necessary to identify its location within educational theory and how it contributes to students' deep learning. Tracing a theoretical paradigm for service-learning is the task of the next chapter. Before embarking on this exploratory journey from an historical perspective, however, a glance at the planned route map reveals that this section of the book will also visit areas such as the definitions, characteristics, principles, and potential outcomes of service-learning.

Historical context

Within higher education, a service-learning course will require students to serve their community for a stipulated period of time, for example, for a set number of hours per week, within the duration of the academic course, which may be one semester or longer. As a requirement of service-learning, therefore, it could be argued that the students' service is not essentially voluntary. Students' activities on placement in the community are, however, akin to voluntary work in that it is unpaid and perceived as meaningful 'service' with an altruistic purpose.

Volunteerism is not a new concept. In Britain, especially during the nineteenth century, philanthropy and humanitarianism were essential factors in sustaining charitable organisations. With the prevalent laissez-faire philosophy at the time, the government did not intervene in the welfare of its citizens. The effects of industrialisation, subsequent urbanisation, and two World Wars contributed to the growth in the ideology of collectivism. This growth or momentum reached its zenith at the end of World War II and is demonstrated by the establishment of the post-war welfare state. The idea of a comprehensive welfare state designed to care for its citizens 'from the cradle to the grave' was guided by the recommendations published in the government command paper Social Insurance and Allied Services (HMSO, 1942), otherwise known as the Beveridge Report. Beveridge's vision of a 'good society' was reflected in a system of universal welfare provided and managed by the state. It could be argued that, unintentionally, this also resulted in a less urgent need for volunteerism. Ironically, volunteerism has regained significance in twenty-first-century Britain, a trend which may well have been germinated subsequent to the retrenchment of welfare in the twentieth century during the Thatcher years.

The role of the state has since changed so that it is no longer the main provider of welfare services in the United Kingdom. In its place there is now a mixed economy of welfare with a larger role for the voluntary sector as a source of welfare provision. Although the voluntary sector has paid employees, one of its defining characteristics is that of unpaid volunteer workers. Consequently, it could be contended that, in the United Kingdom, there are increasing opportunities for people to volunteer. So, service-learning would seem to fit appropriately into this new zeitgeist.

In order to sustain a civil society, it could be argued that there is a need to nurture civic virtues and civic participation. Indeed, voter apathy was evident in the 'declining election turnout – 59% in the 2001 general election (under 40% of 18 to 24s)' (Greenwood and Robins, 2002, p. 510), and fears of declining social capital in the United States (Putnam, 2000) may also become an impending British problem. Encouraging civic engagement through education could help to provide a solution. For example, New Labour emphasised the relevance of active citizenship which could be nurtured through education. The Report of the Commission on Citizenship (1990, pp. 15, xviii) had already endorsed 'Education for Citizenship' and recommended 'that the study and experience of citizenship should be a part of every young person's education ... that each local education authority reviews the range and type of support available for community work and citizenship activities, particularly within the youth service and adult education'.

Influenced by Communitarian ideas of a 'good society' in which the 'common good' is upheld, it could be argued that there were political as well as ideological reasons for New Labour introducing citizenship education as a compulsory subject in the National Curriculum, which became effective in secondary schools in England in 2002. Although not recognised as a single subject as such in the Scottish education curriculum, a concern about citizenship was evident through its identification as a 'priority' in the Standards in Scotland's Schools Act 2000. Furthermore, the Education for Citizenship in Scotland Report (2002) recommended a national framework for the integration of citizenship across the curriculum. The New Labour government's education policy was congruent with the recommendations of a report by the QCA Advisory Group on Citizenship (1998, p. 8), more familiarly known as the Crick Report, which claimed there were 'worrying levels of apathy, ignorance and cynicism about political and public life and also involvement in neighbourhood and community affairs'. Macfarlane (2005, p. 298) added that '[c]oncern about youth alienation from democratic processes has led, at least in part, to the introduction of citizenship education in schools.' Building on this foundation, the Coalition Government in 2010 continued with a focus on citizenship in schools and its message of a 'Big Society', encouraging young people to contribute to the 'common good' by actively participating in their communities through voluntary work. Intrinsic to this are implications for higher education.

The face of higher education changed dramatically over the years through 'massification' following New Labour's activation of their pledge to increase the number of young people in higher education to 50% by 2010 (Labour Party Manifesto, 2005). Consequently, the purpose and nature of higher education has altered. In 1997, the National Committee of Inquiry into Higher Education (NCIHE), otherwise known as the Dearing Report, recommended the development of employability, or transferable skills, and more active participation within the community. This, the report claims, 'may be achieved through work experience, involvement in student union activities, or in work in community or voluntary settings' (NICHE, 1997, sect. 9.26). By active involvement in local communities through acts of volunteering, young people may not only contribute to the good of society, but they may also develop their own skills suitable for employment. It could be argued, of course, that this is also good for society in that it nurtures a stronger workforce. A specific example of how this could be enacted is a project in Scotland that began in 2007 called 'Aiming University Learning @ Work', led by the University of Glasgow in collaboration with the University of St. Andrews and Glasgow Caledonian University. A more general example of how these aims may be met is through service-learning. As Annette (2000a, p. 117) affirms, 'An important way in which students can develop key skills through work experience and experientially realize education for citizenship is through service-learning'. Theoretically, it would appear that service-learning is congruent with the aims of current education policy and the ultimate aim of enabling engaged and active graduate citizens. Service-learning involves community participation, and thus it provides an opportunity to develop citizenship, as 'one of the best ways of putting the theories of citizenship into practice is through voluntary work in the community' (QCA, 1998, p. 61).

From a political and public policy perspective, citizenship is an important issue that, if nurtured and developed, may contribute towards a more civil society. Since the beginning of his term in office, Blair promoted 'civic activism'. He said that '[s]trong communities depend on shared values and a recognition of the rights and duties of citizenship – not just the duty to pay taxes and obey the law, but the obligation to bring up children as competent, responsible citizens' (Blair, in Chadwick and Heffernan, 2003, p. 131). It could be argued, however, that a policy of citizenship education is in the interests of the state in that it can be a form of social control. Alternatively, it can be perceived as being in the interests of the citizen in that a civil society is one in which high levels of trust can be developed among citizens. According to Fitzpatrick (2005, p. 61), there is more stability in higher trust communities, whereas there are 'higher levels of stress, crime, isolation and incivility' in lower trust communities. Whether community engagement or citizenship education is conducive to building trust is debateable. Nonetheless, service-learning, which involves community work, could be understood as a form of 'civic activism'. Certainly, in the literature it is identified as a form of citizenship education, or at least interpreted as a contribution towards encouraging young people to become civically engaged. In this sense, then, service-learning could be seen as a useful educational tool that may have an underlying political agenda. Indeed, in some European countries, it is posited that citizenship education is used to deliberately inculcate particular beliefs to ensure social stability and control (Dimitrov and Boyadjieva, 2009). Ironically, if service-learning is utilised as citizenship education, it may have the opposite effect because, as a consequence of their critical thinking and critical action, students may challenge state control.

The notion of addressing 'social recession' through educational practice focusing on civic and community engagement is not new, nor is it unique to the United Kingdom. How to prepare students most effectively for 'engaged citizenship' has been a salient question in the United States for several decades (Caron et al., 1999). Lisman (1998, p. 23) claims that '[w]idespread support exists for service-learning as one of the ways to promote the civic virtues necessary for creating a more civil society'. It is claimed that service-learning is a method of civic engagement and 'one of the most important strategies for realizing the ideal of an engaged campus' (Hollander and Hartley, 2003, p. 310). Putnam (2000), in his recommendations for civic renewal, also refers to service-learning as one way of achieving this goal. He says that service learning programmes may 'improve civic knowledge, enhance citizen efficacy, increase social responsibility and self-esteem, teach skills of co-operation and leadership, and may even ... reduce racism' (p. 405).

Recognition that service to the community was beneficial in various ways was evident with the founding of the Voluntary Service Overseas (VSO) during the climate of the post-war consensus on welfare. In a letter to *The Sunday Times* in March 1958, Alec and Moira Dickson outlined the benefits of this type of service to youth in their 'gap year', after leaving school but before entry to university. It was believed that this type of experience would be of huge educational benefit to them in addition to their voluntary work being of benefit to the recipients of the service. According to Tonkin (1998, pp. 1–2), Alec Dickson did not differentiate 'between experience and education, and he believed that the one could and should, inform the other'. This concept encapsulates the essence of service-learning. Although the VSO originated in Britain, the idea of international service was arguably more popular in North America with the subsequent introduction of the Peace Corps by President John F. Kennedy and enshrined in law under the Peace Corps Act (Public Law 87–293) 1961. Tonkin (1998) claims that the effects of the war in Vietnam and the politicisation of education led to changes in American tertiary education curricula in order to make it more relevant to the increasing numbers of students. He says that '[u]niversities and colleges began to give credit for unconventional experiential education' (p. 2). In addition, it is asserted that 'service-learning was forged within the fires of the civil rights movement' (Butin, 2010, p. 152). The national Campus Compact in the United States later began in 1985. The aim was to promote students' civic engagement through voluntary work. The growth in this movement became vast, and currently involved in Campus Compact are 'nearly 1,100 college and university presidents – representing (approximately) 5 million students' (http://www.compact.org). The popularity of engagement with, and service to, the community was further embedded in American public policy with the National and Community Service Act 1990 and the National Service Trust Act 1993. Described as a 'reform movement' (Lisman, 1998, p. 24), service-learning became part of the curriculum in American secondary and tertiary education and continues to be popular (Billig, 2001). Such is the belief in its effecting civic virtues in young people that 'several cities, such as Chicago and Philadelphia, either strongly encourage or actually mandate service-learning' in schools (Billig, 2000, p. 659). More recently, volunteerism and service-learning have been actively encouraged by the US president Obama and through the Serve America Act 2009. Many universities that are members of Campus Compact include service-learning as part of their core curriculum within degree courses. Indeed, a survey claimed that 'there was an average of 66 of these courses per campus in 2012' (Campus Compact, 2013).

In Britain, the story is somewhat different in terms of establishing a culture of service-learning, although there has been a similar massive increase in the number of university students, particularly beginning in the period when New Labour was in power, from 1997 to 2010. This has led to a different focus than volunteerism and instead, there is now an emphasis on courses that help to develop students' graduate attributes and employability skills, or skills that are transferable to the workplace. These are becoming increasingly part of the overt intended learning outcomes or objectives of academic courses. An unintended consequence of this is that experiential education is becoming more relevant. Added to this was the Coalition Government's introduction in 2011 of a National Citizen Service that aims to enliven social responsibility in 16- and 17–year-olds by encouraging their participation in voluntary work within their local communities. This is part of Cameron's idea of a 'Big Society', in which it could be argued that service-learning has a niche. In its role as citizenship education, it would appear that service-learning can improve students' sense of social responsibility and development of civic virtues, in addition to enhancing their employability skills and attributes.

The time seems ripe for the wider introduction of service-learning to higher education curricula across the United Kingdom, as at present there are few service-learning courses available. A deeper investigation into service-learning is imperative, however, in order to justify supporting this pedagogical approach and, importantly, to understand the nature of the potential effectiveness of service-learning. This is especially pertinent considering that service-learning is also becoming a global educational phenomenon, gaining increasing popularity in the Asia-Pacific region, for example. As referred to earlier, the concept of service and learning being mutually informative and beneficial is the cornerstone of service-learning. How it is defined, however, is a matter that echoes with the sound of many voices. It is to this vast space that our journey now proceeds.

Definitions of service-learning

Within the literature there appears to be an unending quest for a definitive statement of service-learning as if it were an enigma or a 'holy grail'. There is no universal agreement on one definition of service-learning. Indeed, it has been referred to as a philosophy and a pedagogy, in addition to being an academic course of study and an educational experience (Butin, 2010; Deeley, 2010; Kenworthy-U'Ren, 2003; Anderson, 1998; Mendel-Reyes, 1998). Terms that are interchangeable with service-learning mischievously obscure the trail for a definitive meaning. Examples of such terms include: community volunteer learning; community based learning; service based learning; and community service. The latter, unfortunately, has negative connotations in the United Kingdom because it commonly refers to a type of punishment meted out by Courts of Justice for crime not deemed to deserve a custodial sentence. More hazards also lie en route to the destination of a definitive meaning of 'service-learning' through terminology used for diverse forms of experiential education. Examples of such terms include 'volunteerism', 'internships', 'work placements', and 'field education'. A basic explanation of how these terms differ in meaning resides in the beneficiaries of the activity, for example, the main aim of internships, work placements, vocational or professional courses, and field education is for the benefit of the student. By contrast, the main aim of volunteerism is to benefit the recipient. Service-learning crosses the boundaries because it aims to benefit both the student and the recipient of his or her service in the community (Deeley, 2010; Mendel-Reyes, 1998). As such, service-learning involves mutuality and reciprocity (Deeley, 2004), although reciprocity may vary in degree (Clayton et al., 2010).

   Although it is necessary to have a fundamental understanding of what service-learning means in theory and in practice, it is also pertinent to note that a definitive statement may be restrictive, and as Butin (2010, p. 17) shrewdly points out, 'the request for definitional certainty has the potential to constrain rather than foster emergent practices' (see also Butin, 2003). Butin (2005, p. 98) also claims that service-learning is 'a pedagogy immersed in the complexities and ambiguities of how we come to make sense of ourselves and the world around us'. Furthermore, the opportunity for students to create their own knowledge and understanding through service-learning implies that some outcomes may be 'unintended/unanticipated' (Furco, 2003, p. 16). From this viewpoint, it is understandable that diversity within service-learning programmes is natural and allows for rich and varied experiences for students and a multiplicity of benefits for the communities they serve.

Service-learning is, in a sense, a generic term indicating a particular mode of learning. It lends itself to idiocratic programmes of study that may be inherently unique while having common bonds with other service-learning programmes worldwide. This makes definitive statements not only very difficult, but perhaps also undesirable because the beauty of service-learning lies in its flexibility. A broad statement outlining the fundamental meaning of service-learning is more useful. There are a number of such 'umbrella' definitions that are helpfully wide in the search for its meaning. Jacoby (1996, p. 5) offers a broad definition of service-learning, saying it is 'a form of experiential learning in which students engage in activities that address human and community needs together with structured opportunities intentionally designed to promote student learning and development'. Similarly, Bringle and Hatcher (1996) also offer a definition claiming that service-learning is

> a credit bearing educational experience in which students participate in an organised service activity that meets identified community needs and reflect on the service activity in such a way as to gain further understanding of course content, a broader appreciation of the discipline, and an enhanced sense of civic responsibility. (p. 221)

These statements demonstrate that service-learning is a dual combination of academic learning and service to the community, which is mutually reinforcing and beneficial (Porter Honnet and Poulsen, 1989). In addition, Campus Compact (2013) states that service-learning plays a 'role in educating students for responsible citizenship, strengthening communities, and fulfilling the public purpose of higher education'. Following this search for a clearer understanding of service-learning, it is useful to explore its defining characteristics.

Characteristics of service-learning

From the previous section, it is clear that the key characteristics of service-learning are student learning and civic engagement. Together these aspects connect academia with the community, a factor which is discussed later in this chapter. There are several aspects of service-learning, however, that may be summarised by the requirements that: the service is linked with coursework; student reflection combines service and coursework; the coursework is assessed, but not necessarily the service per se; and the service meets community needs (Butin, 2003; Pritchard, 2001; Weigert, 1998). Various authors augment these factors. Enos and Troppe (1996, p. 72), for example, claim that '[m]ost faculty require students to keep a journal and write a reflective paper that synthesizes the service experience and the course concepts'. In this process it is imperative that students recognise the relevance of their practical service experience in the community to their academic learning and vice versa (Eyler, 2000). The combination of academic coursework and service in the community are, therefore, essential characteristics of service-learning (Billig and Welch, 2004). The connections between theory and practice are vital to service-learning, and the route to making these connections is through critical reflection.

Kenworthy-U'Ren (2003, p. 52) usefully identifies a number of key elements that characterise service-learning, which include 'a focus on real world learning...a course-based foundation...reciprocity between the student and the community; and...carefully designed reflection'. To clarify so far, service-learning involves students' service to the community and their engagement in reflection on this activity, which involves connecting it to the academic component of the course.

There are further components of service-learning that are discussed in the literature. Bringle and Hatcher (1996, p. 221), for example, refer to civic responsibility as another dimension of service-learning. They suggest that service-learning encourages students to become responsible citizens, an idea that is reinforced by Campus Compact (2013). The notion of developing students'

'civic responsibility' is one of the recurring themes in the literature on service-learning. This supports an assertion that service-
learning in higher education contributes to developing students'
graduate attributes. Another related theme includes that of the
creation and development of partnerships between university and
the community (Caron et al., 1999; Vernon and Ward, 1999; Jacoby
and Associates, 2003). Butin (2003, p. 1674) outlines the aims of
service-learning in terms of broad outcomes that include a connection between university and the community and overall to 'foster a
more active citizenry'. Herein lie political and ideological agendas
because there is an ultimate goal of the promotion of a 'more equi-
table society' (p. 1675). Mendel-Reyes (1998, p. 37) clearly argues
that service-learning inherently involves citizenship, saying that
'[t]hrough service learning, students improve their abilities to
participate in democratic deliberation'. Hollander and Hartley
(2003, p. 310) echo this perspective by asking a rhetorical question: 'What better way of reasserting the role of service-learning in
higher education than by dedicating it to the purpose of renewing
our democracy?' It is interesting that equity and democracy are
highlighted in relation to service-learning, although there is
an assumption that these factors are only applicable outside the
classroom. Recent research paves the way, however, to embedding
these factors within the pedagogical structure of service-learning
and through collaborative and summative assessment methods
(Deeley, 2014). Thus far, it is evident that in service-learning there
is a further agenda of promoting societal change. Indeed, action
that is taken for this purpose is claimed by Cipolle (2010, p. 5) to
be 'critical' and 'a distinct subset of service-learning', which echoes
the view of Mitchell (2008) who distinguishes between 'traditional'
and 'critical' models of service-learning.

It is not uncommon for education to be used as a political means,
indeed, it is claimed that all education is political (Freire, 1970).
McLaren (2003, p. 178) is explicit in his view that '[s]chools must
become sites for the production of both critical knowledge and socio-
political action. Any institution worthy of the appellation "school"
must educate students to become active agents for social transformation and critical citizenship.' This echoes the critical pedagogy
developed by Freire (1970), which is discussed in the next chapter.
Mendel-Reyes (1998, p. 32) also believes that education can instigate

both individual and political change, with service-learning having a key role to 'revitalize citizenship education and citizenship itself'. This perspective could be interpreted as a way in which academia can benefit the community and thus 'serve societal needs' (Anderson, 2005, p. 38) by providing education that enables civic responsibility. These ideas are also endorsed by others (Bringle and Clayton, 2012; Rubin, 2000; Weigert, 1998) and interpreted as a 'cultural' perspective of service-learning (Butin, 2010, p. 9).

Intrinsic to a civic agenda, there are underlying and implicit goals. It is not clear, however, whether the socio-political perspective is an optional addition to the aims of service-learning; whether service-learning offers a convenient vehicle for a socio-political agenda; or whether this type of learning naturally results in students' increased socio-political awareness or activity. Nevertheless, Butin (2010, p. 10) observes that service-learning accommodates a 'political' perspective. If service-learning is perceived as having radical or 'subversive' goals, however, this potential agenda might add grist to potential resistance to its wider introduction in more traditional higher education institutions.

Principles of service-learning

For deeper insight into what service-learning entails, it is useful to explore its 'principles' as categorised in the literature. Not dissimilar to other 'movements', or collections of ideas, service-learning has been encapsulated within sets of principles, which are typically presented as numbered lists. Undoubtedly, there is some value in this because principles can offer guidance to service-learning practitioners by offering statements of theory and good practice. This could be interpreted as encapsulating a 'technical' perspective of service learning (Butin, 2010, p. 8). The Wingspread Special Report (Johnson Foundation, 1989), for example, identified ten principles as criteria for service-learning programmes. One of these principles claims that effective service-learning '[p]rovides structured opportunities for people to reflect critically on their service experience' (pp. 2–3). Similarly, the National Society for Internships and Experiential Education (NSIEE) compiled a list of ten principles of good practice which includes reference to 'clear service and learning goals for everyone involved' and 'to program participation by and with diverse populations' (Kendall and Associates, 1990, pp. 37–55). Interestingly, there is no mention of civic responsibility, citizenship, or developing students' socio-political awareness. From another perspective, Sigmon (1990, p. 57) offers a set of three principles, which are 'those being served control the service(s) provided...Those being served become better able to serve and be served by their own actions...Those who serve also are learners and have significant control over what is expected to be learned.' This brings another dimension to the meaning of service-learning in that the focus here is on community empowerment.

Tonkin (1998) provides a list of nine principles of service-learning, which offer further insight to the goals of service-learning. Interestingly, he claims that people 'working in a service-learning environment become better teachers'. This idea is echoed by Bowen (2005, p. 14) who states that 'university faculty and students experience the rich teaching and learning benefits that accrue to service-learning participants', although it is not clear what these benefits are or how they occur. Research in to this particular area of service-learning would be beneficial and could inform university teachers' professional development. Tonkin (1998) also refers to the notion of social change by stating that 'students make practical contributions to relieve others' suffering and to enlarge others' opportunities', which also relates to empowerment.

Enos and Troppe (1996) assert that the basic principle of service-learning is students' service to the community and their reflections on this. Action and reflection are both vital. Mintz and Hesser (1996), on the other hand, emphasise the principles of collaboration and reciprocity in service-learning. These aspects can refer to relationships concerning students, the recipients of service, the professional service providers, and teachers. On a structural level, service-learning certainly implies a relationship between the university and the community, an issue which is critically investigated by Clayton et al. (2010).

Outcomes of service-learning

It is possible to arrive at a deeper understanding of service-learning by examining its outcomes or effects. Service-learning has been referred to as a 'pedagogical tool' (Kenworthy-U'Ren,

2003) to secure the aim of increased civic responsibility through community engagement and academic learning. It is claimed that an enhanced sense of citizenship results from service-learning (Deeley, 2007; Butin, 2003; Hollander and Hartley, 2003; Mendel-Reyes, 1998; Bringle and Hatcher, 1996). There is, however, a vast array of claims to what students can achieve further through this form of experiential learning. One aspect is increased intellectual skills (Deeley, 2007; Tonkin, 2004; Bringle and Hatcher, 1996; Batchelder and Root, 1994). Other aspects include: increased potential for socio-political activity (Cipolle, 2010; Mitchell, 2008; Rocha, 2000; Mendel-Reyes, 1998); a change in students' 'attitudes and values related to diversity, poverty, justice, social change, and inequality' (Bowman et al., 2010, p. 26); and it is claimed that there is accelerated personal development (Giles and Eyler, 1994a) with the potential for transformational changes to occur (Deeley, 2010). Miller et al. (2002, p. 200) state that '[f]rom a theoretical viewpoint, service-learning would appear to facilitate not only academic achievement, but also critical thinking, character development, social relationships, self-esteem, citizenship, and cultural awareness'. Bringle and Hatcher (1996, p. 221) reinforce this view, claiming that service-learning has a 'positive impact on personal, attitudinal, moral, social, and cognitive outcomes', a view shared by Astin et al. (2000). In addition, service-learning offers ample opportunities for students to develop employability skills and graduate attributes (Deeley, 2014).

The main effects of service-learning that have been identified in the literature can be broadly categorised into three groups. Firstly, the effects can be an enhanced sense of citizenship. In this category, increased civic engagement and greater potential for socio-political activity are included. Secondly, the effects may involve accelerated intellectual development. Thirdly, personal development may occur.

Citizenship

Relevant to the discourse on citizenship are the civic virtues of civility, trust, public spiritedness, active participation and engagement. Of these, Toole (2001, p. 57) believes that '[s]ocial trust may be particularly important to service-learning because it is a "relationship-rich" pedagogy', and adds that service-learning is therefore a 'potentially powerful tool to foster civil society'. Indeed, civic engagement and education are important in service-learning (Bringle and Clayton, 2012), and this type of experiential learning may contribute positively to the development of the knowledge, skills, attitudes, behaviour, and intentions of students to become effective and civically engaged citizens (Billig and Welch, 2004). Moreover, participating in service-learning may foster students' commitment to future service long after their academic course is over (Deeley, 2007; Kearney, 2004; Eyler, 2000), although it is valid to point out that students may already be inclined to continue volunteering after the course has finished (Moely et al., 2008). Service-learning may contribute to what has been referred to as 'social capital', which, according to Putnam (2000), is disappearing. Butin (2003, p. 1674) reinforces this idea by saying that service-learning is a 'means of re-engaging today's youth with both academics and civic values'. Other studies also reiterate one of the benefits of service-learning as civic renewal (Butin, 2003; Hollander and Hartley, 2003). Moreover, by offering 'an opportunity to examine social justice issues in a real world context' (McHatton et al., 2006, p. 68) service-learning allows students' greater awareness and involvement in the community. Similarly, Giles and Eyler (1994a, p. 327) regard service-learning students as 'participating citizens of the community'. Indeed, service-learning has been referred to as a 'pedagogy for citizenship' (Mendel-Reyes, 1998, p. 34), a view echoed by others (Kenworthy-U'Ren, 2003; Rubin, 2000; Lisman, 1998). Furthermore, it is asserted that service-learning can nurture racial tolerance as well as enhancing civic responsibility (Howard, 2003).

Controversially, service-learning has been perceived as having the potential to increase students' participation in socio-political activity. For some of its critics, service-learning could be regarded as a subversive tool and a consequence of indoctrination. In contrast, others may perceive service-learning as a benign process of increasing students' critical awareness. If service-learning was in part responsible for students' socio-political activities, it could be perceived as being contrary to the aim of education policy, if that policy contained an agenda of social control (Dimitrov and Boyadjieva, 2009), as referred to earlier. Of course, students may be inclined to participate in socio-political activity regardless of service-learning (Dreuth and Dreuth-Fewell, 2002).

According to the service-learning literature, this pedagogical approach appears to be compatible with the aims of citizenship education through the nurturing of civic virtues and increasing the civic engagement of students. A major incentive for its introduction in higher education, however, is the claim that service-learning enhances students' learning (Warren, 2012).

Intellectual development

A vital factor in the development of intellectual skills in service-learning is critical thinking (Deeley, 2010; Giles and Eyler, 1998; Batchelder and Root, 1994). Indeed, Mendel-Reyes (1998, p. 37) refers to 'service-learning' as 'a pedagogy for critical thinking' with the potential to nurture life-long learning (Rubin, 2000). By linking theory to practice, service-learning deepens students' learning (Kenworthy-U'Ren, 2003; Eyler, 2000; Piper et al., 2000). It is also conducive to critical thinking and problem analysis (Kearney, 2004). Miller (1994) explains that these metacognitive factors can be attributed to the combination of students' analysis of abstract concepts, contained within the associated academic course, with students' critical reflection on their service experiences. Similarly, Bringle and Hatcher (1996, p. 221) claim that service-learning students have 'shown higher academic performance in exams'. Service-learning can enhance students' oral and written skills (Howard, 2003; Astin et al., 2000; Mendel-Reyes, 1998; Lisman, 1998) and through specifically designed assessment methods, can further help to develop students' employability skills and attributes (Deeley, 2014), which is discussed in Chapter 7.

Personal development

So far, it has been claimed that service-learning may enhance students' civic engagement and intellectual skills. It is further claimed, however, that students' personal growth can also be facilitated by the experiential element in service-learning as it can facilitate the role of emotion in learning (Langstraat and Bowdon, 2011). This can lead to personal growth, which is a result of combining 'cognitive with...affective (factors)' (Butin, 2005, p. vii).

Many studies have claimed that service-learning increases the social and personal development of students (Deeley, 2010; Kearney, 2004; Astin et al., 2000; Billig, 2000; Eyler, 2000; Mendel-Reyes,

1998; Driscoll et al., 1996). There are a number of factors with regard to personal development or development of graduate attributes. Eyler (2000), for example, believes that service-learning has a positive impact on interpersonal skills. It can also enhance the effectiveness of students' 'communication and social interaction, (and) decision-making' (Kearney, 2004, p. 9). Increased self-confidence, self-esteem, leadership skills, and social awareness can be developed through service-learning (Howard, 2003; Lisman, 1998; Batchelder and Root, 1994). There is a risk, however, that service-learning may lose its credibility through a lack of empirical evidence to support these claims and by its becoming a 'win-win mantra' (Butin, 2003, p. 1679). There is also a lack of criticality in the assumptions that service-learning invariably is beneficial for students; that they are intellectually ready for this type of learning experience (Perry, 1999); and that service-learning is always a positive experience. Overall in the literature, there is a dearth of critical analysis of the more difficult, or negative, aspects of service-learning, although some cast light on its potentially shadier aspects (Deeley, 2014, 2010; Jones et al., 2005; Jones, 2002).

Negative aspects

Cynically, Lally (2001, p. 55) says that the 'accolades bestowed upon service-learning by its proponents range from the aesthetic to the weighty, and the moral to the cerebral'. By contrast, there are more critical perspectives of service-learning (Deeley, 2014, 2010; Jones et al., 2005; Jones, 2002). Jones (2002) reveals a negative aspect of service-learning and challenges claims to the inevitability of its benefits. Jones et al. (2005) further examine this issue and claim that not all students inevitably benefit from participating in service-learning. They describe its negative aspect in terms of the 'underside' of service-learning and illustrate this in terms of students' resistance, from being discontented to 'active resisters'. The root of the problem lies with the difficulties students experience in attempting to make connections between academic theory and the 'real world'. As a result, students may become frustrated with this difficult task and reject service-learning altogether. Jones et al. (2005) attribute students' resistance to the intellectual challenges that service-learning provides. It is possible that such students are not at an appropriate cognitive level (Perry, 1999) for the type of learning that is involved in service-learning. In this case, service-learning may be more appropriate for students in their more senior academic years. Paradoxically, student resistance may be interpreted as a form of engagement (Cooks and Scharrer, 2006) and resistance arising from students' negative service experiences has transmuted into positive learning experiences (Deeley, 2007). The studies by Jones (2002) and Jones et al. (2005) provide a critical perspective by acknowledging that not all students necessarily benefit from service-learning. They also demonstrate that the outcomes of service-learning cannot always be predicted, which is a salient aspect exemplified and reinforced by Deeley (2010).

Conclusion

This chapter has contextualised service-learning historically, examined its fundamental characteristics and principles, and summarily explored its potential outcomes. It is evident that there are many claims to the benefits of service-learning; however, the thorny issues of how and why these occur are not explicitly evident. As Mabry (1998, p. 32) confirms, '[W]e know little about the practices that contribute to these outcomes'. This is poignantly reiterated by Billig and Eyler (2003, p. 259), who say that service-learning is not 'maximised' 'since the learning theory is often not well articulated or understood by service-learning practitioners'. There is little convincing evidence of its efficacy, particularly in the light of the diversity of service-learning programmes and the inherent variables of service experience. The lack of credible theory to underpin the efficacy of service-learning has been acknowledged (Warren, 2012), but the concern in much of the literature is on theories that can be tested in a scientific mode, applying quantitative research methods. It can be argued, however, that where human subjects are concerned in educational endeavours, qualitative research methods, or mixed methods using quantitative and qualitative approaches, are more effective.

Much of the literature ascribes the success of this pedagogy to the depth or quality of learning that it instigates. The crucial question of how learning takes place is less evident in the literature. To discover the reasons why there may be certain effects of service-learning on students, it is necessary to turn to other sources and bodies of literature, which will be the focus of the next chapter. According to quality assurance requirements in higher education in the United Kingdom, it is imperative that aims and intended learning outcomes of teaching and academic courses are aligned to and can be measured or graded through assessment. This poses a major problem where service-learning is concerned if teachers are unaware of how effective learning might best be facilitated and what that learning actually entails, especially in relation to the students' unforeseeable experiences on placement. When expounding the virtues of service-learning, it is worth bearing in mind that 'any theory and set of practices is dogmatic which is not based upon critical examination of its own underlying principles' (Dewey, 1938, p. 10). At this point, therefore, it is politic to raise anchor and henceforth sail on to Chapter 3 in search of an appropriate theoretical paradigm to secure a reliable and valid haven for service-learning.

3
A Theoretical Paradigm for Service-Learning

Introduction

The previous chapter was a metaphorical tour exploring different explanations of service-learning in an attempt to understand the nature of this pedagogy. In some respects, it would be fair to say that service-learning might be regarded as an umbrella term to denote diverse and multidisciplinary learning activities that are bound together by common characteristics and key component features. These components, within a structured framework, invariably consist of: academic coursework, practical service experience or voluntary work, critical reflection, tutorial group discussion, and journal writing. The practical service experiences, however, are often ill-structured and the learning from them opaque to students. It is important, therefore, that teachers facilitate students' structured critical reflection because by relating practical experiences to theoretical aspects of the academic coursework, students can begin to comprehend how their service and learning meshed together are epigenetic and mutually informative.

There is an enormous amount of energy placed in research endeavours attempting to 'prove' that service-learning is an effective pedagogy that can achieve its various intended learning outcomes. This plethora of literature extols the positive outcomes of service-learning, but offers very little explanation of how the learning outcomes are achieved (Butin, 2010). Establishing a viable educational foundation for service-learning, however, may sharpen the focus of this type of pedagogical research away from attempts to 'prove it works' towards a more sustainable approach of improving how it works. This chapter, therefore, stems from a rejection of a positivist approach and, instead, turns attention to a feasible framework for service-learning in order to secure and justify its potential efficacy. The aim is to provide an informed theoretical paradigm for service-learning by drawing on extant, relevant, and multiple theories. In so doing, this chapter investigates and expounds the educational rationale and value underlying service-learning practice. It is an attempt to fill a gap in the current literature as there is a commonly unquestioned assumption that there is only one source of service-learning, with its conceptual origins being invariably attributed solely to Dewey's educational philosophy (Giles and Eyler, 1994b). This is not to deny that his writings offer remarkable insight into its educational basis. Despite his influence on experiential learning and reflective thinking, however, Dewey did not refer to service-learning per se, as this term did not emerge until 1967. From a more critical perspective and deeper analysis, it is possible to identify further sources that contribute to the influences on service-learning and its success in facilitating students' deep learning. It is these sources that provide, in addition to Dewey's philosophy, a more inclusive and broader theoretical paradigm for service-learning. Encapsulating the core reasoning and theoretical grounding of service-learning would help to sustain its educational integrity and perhaps rescue it from its 'marginal status' (Liu, 1995, p. 16) on the periphery of mainstream education or, indeed its invisibility in many higher education institutions in the United Kingdom.

The quest for a theoretical paradigm for service-learning will begin firstly by exploring the nature of this type of learning and how it occurs. Learning will be interpreted here as making meaning from experience and thus will draw on personal construct theory analysis. In the light of this, an understanding of how we make sense of our world through thought and language will be explored first, drawing ideas from Vygotsky. Experiential learning theory and the concept of an experiential learning cycle are essential to the purpose of this chapter. As the book concerns service-learning in the context of higher education it is also pertinent that adult learning theory is encapsulated within this paradigm, as well as the notion of collaborative learning in a democratic classroom. Similarly, there is also a niche for transformative learning theory within which key concepts blend with those in service-learning. Aspects of transformative learning theory will be explored further in Chapter 4.

Making meaning

It could be argued that meaning is central to understanding and learning. Learning, however, could be perceived as the discrete acquisition of facts, as advocated by the character of Thomas Gradgrind in *Hard Times* (Dickens, 1854). In this novel, the teacher is described as 'a kind of cannon loaded to the muzzle with facts, and prepared to blow (the pupils) clean out of the regions of childhood at one discharge' (p. 9). The differentiation between learning that involves meaning and learning that focuses on particular pieces of information has been made in terms of Svensson's idea of holistic and atomistic approaches to learning (Marton and Säljö, 1984). Learning that involves meaning tends to be recalled more easily and has long lasting effects (Bligh, 1972). By contrast, an atomistic or surface approach to learning is quite often a strategy adopted for examination purposes, or, in Gradgrind's methodology, for the regurgitation of facts and figures, as commonly evident in traditional learning and teaching. Most of such knowledge is invariably forgotten following a time lapse (Boyatzis et al., in Harvey and Knight, 1996, p. 152), who report that 'six weeks after taking an exam, students retained only about 40 per cent of the material'. Service-learning, however, embraces holistic learning for meaning. An investigation into this, and how it contributes to a theoretical paradigm, involves a preliminary exploration of thought and language as this is vital to the making of meaning.

Thought and language

There is a relationship between thought and language (Dewey, 1933; Vygotsky, 1962). Language may be needed for thought or, at least, to express one's thoughts and to communicate them to others. Understanding, or making meaning, involves thought, but it could be posited that language is essential to this process. Thought is amorphous and to give it substance, it must be captured through a medium. The focus here is on language, although it could be argued that there are various other media, for example, art or photography. To articulate meaning through spoken or written words entails a process of expression through one's vocabulary. This may clarify or obfuscate the complexity of meaning, but it also suggests that thought and understanding could be limited by the extent of our vocabulary. To make meaning or to understand, there is some necessity to combine the physical world with the world of inchoate thought. Here a connection with service-learning is apparent in that there is mirrored a combination of material and ephemeral spheres. Students are required to reflect critically (which involves ephemeral thought) on their service to the community (which involves the physical world), the links to their associated academic coursework (which involves ephemeral thought and theory) and to express their understanding through language (which involves verbal and written communication through a physical medium).

Learning, according to Dewey (1933, p. 176), 'is not learning things, but the meanings of things, and this process involves the use of signs, or language in its generic sense'. For understanding, we need to know, through experience, what particular words signify. Words can, of course, be used without knowledge of their meaning, indeed without any particular meaning at all, and thus it becomes jargon or 'scholastic cant' (p. 184). There are popular trends of fashionable words, for example, 'that mean almost nothing, deliberately vague but with an illusion of specificity' (BBC, 2012). Eloquently, Dewey (1933, p. 177) says that this 'gives the conceit of learning and coats the mind with a varnish waterproof to new ideas'. What is vital to the learning process, according to Dewey, is that students are enabled to make meaning through language by relating it to their understanding of their own experienced realities. Unfortunately, much of the traditional learning and teaching methods found in higher education institutions frequently rely on transference of facts through the large and didactic lecture format. This process reinforces students' passivity and teaches them 'to live in two separate worlds, one the world of out-of-school experience, the other the world of books and lessons' (p. 200).

Although thought requires language to give it shape and form in order to be communicated to others, it does not imply that thought necessarily requires language. Indeed, pre-linguistic children, and animals that do not have language, have thoughts or experience thought processes. Interestingly, Vygotsky (1962) believes that there are various planes of thought. One of these is of internal language, which may or may not be different to the spoken word. Another plane is where thought occurs devoid of language. A conscious effort to attain this plane of thought can be through meditative practice but to communicate language-less thoughts still requires language or other medium. Inevitably, this can lead to restricted or misconstrued communication of the abstract and amorphous 'reality' of this plane of thought. Language does not always suffice, therefore, to express thought because in capturing thought, language confines its abstract qualities to sometimes inadequate and narrow meaning. Vygotsky uses an effective metaphor to highlight the difficulties in communicating ideas by commenting that '[t]he structure of speech does not simply mirror the structure of thought; that is why words cannot be put on by thought like a ready-made garment' (p. 126).

Thought and language, therefore, can be separate for different reasons. Connections between thought and language can develop because of human maturation and can become more sophisticated through the process of critical and reflective social discourse. This is a vital factor and an essential activity in service-learning. It is essential that students relate the experiences of their service in the community to others in an effort to make meaning in relation to, and in conjunction with, their thoughts, responses, and theoretical academic coursework. Within this context, other service-learning students can offer insight into meaning by providing different and critical perspectives. As such, small discussion groups can nurture students' ability to make meaning from their experiences. These groups can develop into learning communities, where there can be high levels of trust and support, which also provide fertile ground for student friendships to blossom (Deeley, 2010).

Vygotsky believes that individuals are situated at a level of development, while simultaneously having a degree of potential to develop further. This is referred to as the 'zone of proximal development' (Cole et al., 1978, p. 84). He claims that this is unique to humankind and is not possessed by non-human animals. Vygotsky explains that 'human learning presupposes a specific social nature and a process by which children grow into the intellectual life of those around them' (Cole et al., 1978, p. 88). He believes that education should aim to provide the opportunities for children to stretch, metaphorically, to reach their potential. Similarly, the concept of a zone of proximal development could be applied to adult learning. It is possible that small interactive tutorials in higher education can provide an opportunity for growth within students' zones of proximal development.

Although Vygotsky was influenced by Piagetian psychological theory of stages of child development, he differs from Piaget in the explanation of the nature of these stages. Piaget, for example, attributes universal stages of human development to biological urges. By contrast, Vygotsky highlights the importance of the effects of the social environment on human development. This idea is particularly pertinent to service-learning. By combining and inter-relating academic coursework with practical service experience in the community, service-learning concerns a combination of, and interaction between, the internal and abstract mental landscape with the external and material world. This reflects the belief that learning, making meaning, and understanding involve the interaction between individuals and society. Together, they form a 'dialogical process' (Cole et al., 1978, p. 126). Learning can be perceived as a process of enculturation because it is situated in, and part of, culture. This suggests that humans are subject to their place in society, which has vast implications with regard to history, geographical location, class, gender, dis/ability, 'race', and sexual orientation. From a Piagetian perspective, children develop from a concrete and material view of the world, ultimately to an abstract constructionist view. The learning process inextricably concerns the interaction between the individual and his or her environment. In other words, abstract thought must be connected or applied to our experience within the material world to enable us to construct meaning. As our experience affects our thinking, it is plausible to assert that the process of thought and action is mutually reciprocal. All this is relevant to service-learning, as students share their experiences and ideas in class. This encourages them to construct meaning that can be captured in the written narratives of their reflective journals.

Although Vygotsky examines psychological processes of children, they are equally applicable to adults especially when he refers to the internalisation of external events. Experiences occur on two levels: firstly, in the physical, social world; and secondly, in the abstract, private world of the mind. Our thoughts are influenced by our environment, or by society, and they are communicated through our cultural language. Language is a tool used to communicate our thoughts and as this is culturally transmitted, we are inevitably bound within its limitations. This idea is reflected by Burr (1995, p. 35), who says that the 'way language is structured ... determines the way that experience and consciousness are structured'. Accordingly, Vygotsky claims that '[i]f one changes the tools of thinking available to a child, his mind will have a radically different structure' (Cole et al., 1978, p. 126). This is relevant to a theoretical paradigm for service-learning as students are exposed to a different type of learning which can result in raising their awareness. Subsequently, students' behaviour, or action, may change or have the potential to effect change within society. This augments the notion that service-learning can have transformative effects, not only on individuals, but also on society.

Enabling the growth of consciousness is the awareness that thought and language are culturally influenced and transmitted. To explore this aspect further it is useful to investigate the concepts of personal and social constructionism, which are also relevant to a theoretical paradigm for service-learning.

Social constructionism

Social constructionism, or social construct theory, is a valuable component within the theoretical framework of service-learning. Included here is also the notion of personal construct theory, which concerns how people understand or make sense of their personal experiences. As students aim to make meaning from the combination of their experiences and academic coursework through critical reflection, it becomes apparent that they may challenge and deconstruct their assumptions about themselves and their understanding of the world.

Social constructionism concerns the belief that 'reality' is in the 'eye of the beholder' rather than being an independent fact. As Berger and Luckmann (1967, p. 13) claim, '[R]eality is socially constructed' and, as such, is in opposition to positivism. In the light of this perspective, it could be seen that every individual plays a top billing role in the cast of the soap opera of his or her own mind. Our understanding of the world depends upon a myriad of influences: social, cultural, economic, political, and historical. Vygotsky believes that learning is based in, and occurs through, the social world and our interactions with it. This concerns the notion of non-dualism, which indicates a reciprocal relationship between the learner and the environment. As Burr (1995, p. 4) asserts, '[K]nowledge is sustained by social processes' and is exemplified by its transference through language. As individuals are born into these social processes with language already extant, what is learned in early life can become internalised and thus taken for granted. As Bourdieu (in Grenfell and James, 1998, p. 43) eloquently explains, '[W]hen habitus encounters a social world of which it is the product, it finds itself "as a fish in water", it does not feel the weight of the water and takes the world about itself for granted'. It is usually assumed that meaning is shared and that we adopt meanings that have already been given to external phenomena. We learn from others in society and invariably are influenced by others' reactions. In sum, we are social animals. From this aspect, we can learn to typify and stereotype; our expectations can become self-fulfilling prophecies. Indeed, Berger and Luckmann (1967, p. 48) say that 'social structure is the sum total of these typifications and of the recurrent patterns of interaction established by means of them'. Society thus becomes our 'reality'. The social world, however, is constructed by humankind. Similarly, individuals can project their own meaning and create their own 'reality'. So, there is a 'process by which the socially constructed word is internalized in individual consciousness' (p. 91). This reflects a duality of consciousness of being in and of the world, to which Freire (1970) also refers. To maintain a sense of 'reality', it can be argued that interaction with others is essential, which implies that isolation might induce a sense of unreality. Berger and Luckmann (1967, p. 171) believe that '[r]eality-maintenance and reality-confirmation ... involve the totality of the individual's social situation', of which language is an essential communication tool. This is relevant for service-learning as students make sense of their individual experiences on placement through critical dialogue with others in class.

From this socially constructed world, personal constructs abound. We each differentiate between events and phenomena. As Bannister and Fransella (1971, p. 22) explain, 'Each of us lives in what is ultimately a unique world, because it is uniquely interpreted and thereby uniquely experienced'. If, however, we were to perceive and understand the world truly from another's perspective, then our world could be transformed. Bannister and Fransella disagree with Piagetian theory of universal stages of human development in which the world is constructed, because this theory maintains a dualism between material and conceptual worlds. Social constructionism and personal construct theory maintain a belief in non-dualism, that is, the world and how we perceive it are interconnected. We may, of course, alter our constructs but this is no easy task. Kelly (1970, p. 2) refers to this as 'constructive alternativism'. It is possible to challenge our ideas, but others are necessary to help us in this process and 'even the most obvious occurrences of everyday life might appear utterly transformed if we were inventive enough to construe them differently' (p. 1). Essential to the task of raising our awareness and becoming critical thinkers is challenging our assumptions in both the personal and public spheres. Service-learning can provide the forum for this in a search for meaning as students share their practical service experiences with each other and in discussion of academic coursework. When theory and practice do not synchronise, there is an opportunity for learning. This is due to '[d]evelopment (which) can be seen as occurring largely when anticipations fail' (Bannister and Fransella, 1971, p. 87). It is the juxtaposition of what is expected and what transpires that can create imbalance, disharmony, or disjuncture (Jarvis, 2012a, p. 25) which may create a critical point to stimulate learning. Moments such as these may be recorded as 'critical incidents' in service-learning and avail students of the opportunity to make meaning, especially if these incidents are shared in critical discourse with fellow students in the supportive and emotionally safe environment of a reflective tutorial facilitated by a compassionate teacher. As Fransella (1970, p. 65) believes, '[T]he expectancies of a group may act as validators of each individual's personal constructs'. Ideally, this is part of the reflective process in service-learning tutorials. It is also a holistic approach, involving the whole person, in what Lave and Wenger (1991, in Brockbank and McGill, 2007) refer to as the 'process of becoming'. This resonates with Barnett's (1997) perspective that the aims of higher education ought to nurture students' critical being through the preliminary processes of critical thinking and critical action. Service-learning necessitates students to interact with the environment through their service in the community and, because of the experiential nature of this type of learning, allows them the opportunity to become critical individuals who may challenge assumptions in their personally and socially constructed worlds. Before moving on to examine experiential learning theory, it is pertinent to look at some aspects of collaborative learning that can nurture and enhance students' personal constructs and understanding.

Collaborative learning

Collaborative learning concerns social and democratic processes within the classroom and involves interaction and a sharing of power between students and teachers. It is a form of active learning being encouraged and supported in higher education (Cook-Sather et al., 2014; Bovill and Bulley, 2011). Collaborative learning is relevant to a theoretical paradigm for service-learning because students are necessarily involved in a process of shared reflective thinking within a small group tutorial setting. In this context, the teacher may take a leadership role in order to maintain a structure to the students' deliberations in the class. The teacher might also share in the experience of service-learning by participating in service to the community alongside, or at the same time as, the students, although other work commitments may prohibit this. Collaboration can take diverse forms and be evident at varying levels, for example, it may depend on the extent to which the teacher is prepared to relinquish his or her role as the 'authority' or 'expert'. It is firmly tied to ideas of students' active learning, sharing, responsibility, and, ultimately, a democratic classroom. Integral to collaborative learning is student assessment, which is an aspect considered more fully in Chapters 6 and 7. In service-learning, students' learning is grounded in and emerges from their own experience and the dialogical processes within a democratic classroom, rather than from formal teaching. Collaborative learning, therefore, plays a significant role within a theoretical paradigm for service-learning. To begin to understand this and the importance of a democratic classroom, it is useful to explore and contrast the implications of traditional with progressive pedagogy, as well as the role of the teacher.

Traditional pedagogy

D.H. Lawrence (1971, p. 92) observed critically that the purpose of education was the 'leading forth the natural intelligence of the child. But ours is just the opposite of leading forth. It is a ramming in of brain facts through the head, and a consequent distortion, suffocation, and starvation of the primary centres of consciousness'. In this assertion, Lawrence reveals distaste for the didactic transference of information from teacher to student, or what Freire (1970, p. 53) called the 'banking concept' of education. In 'banking' education, teachers make deposits of information in the learner's bank of knowledge. The learner makes withdrawals from this knowledge bank account when required, for example, in assessment exercises. Similarly, Dickens (1854, p. 8) satirically refers to school children as 'little vessels then and there arranged in order, ready to have imperial gallons of facts poured into them until they were full to the brim'.

Traditional teaching and learning is authoritarian and invariably assumes that the transference of knowledge is from an 'expert' to a 'novice'. The process requires 'novices' to be passive recipients of knowledge, who, subsequently, regurgitate their acquired knowledge in academic assignments, which is then assessed by the 'expert' for its accurate recall. This process confirms the power of the 'expert'. Traditionally, students experience limited choice in their curriculum, even within higher education. Here, choices may be made within a range of courses, but rarely is there any choice with regard to educational materials, classroom exercises, or the type of assessment in which they will engage.

It can be argued that education is a social process and that knowledge transference is a traditional part of that process. As a result, we are socialised within our educational experience. Constructs can be made on our behalf by those in power, which suggests that education can be utilised as a form of social control. Indeed, the National Curriculum in England and Wales, as introduced by a Conservative government through the Education Reform Act 1988, established state central control over the content of what was to be taught in schools. It is through traditional pedagogy that the prevailing hegemony can be maintained. Educational hegemony 'reproduces dominant class ideologies and power relationships by privileging certain knowledge and behaviours through course content, instructional practices, and a hidden curriculum' (Matthews, 2005, p. 98). Assumptions concerning the status quo and internalisation of what are socially acceptable behaviours and beliefs can be embedded through this traditional genre. As a result, culture and education together play a very influential role in shaping the character of individuals (Tolstoy, in Spring, 1975). An authoritarian classroom, however, stifles individual choice in learning and the product is a learned passivity, devoid of originality. Traditional education can serve to reinforce existing social structures and maintain individuals' insensitivity to its pervasive influences (Illich, 1971). In this sense, traditional education can be perceived as stifling and dehumanising.

Progressive pedagogy

In contrast, non-traditional education or progressive pedagogy seeks to allow learners the opportunity to be a source of their own knowledge through their active learning. Service-learning fits this model, which is a move away from the didactic and authoritarian teacher-as-expert model towards a more democratic and collaborative means of learning and teaching where students are aroused from their induced passivity. This awakening lights the path towards critical thinking or 'thinking outside the box' (Deeley, 2010, p. 51). As such, progressive pedagogy can be perceived as liberatory or emancipatory education, where raised awareness and, ultimately, critical consciousness can be achieved. The dawning of critical consciousness can provide the catalyst for change and is fertile ground for praxis, where students' independent and critical thought may pave the way to critical action, which ultimately may result in societal changes. As Spring (1975, p. 65) explains, '[A] person who has no consciousness of self, who has nothing but life activity, is completely propelled by social forces. But the person who is aware of these forces and conscious of their nature is able to break with the trajectory of history and participate in the radical change of self and society'.

Shor (1992) also believes that progressive education would effect changes in society. He says that '[c]ritical learning is by itself a form of social action because of its transforming potential, its challenge to the dominant culture inside and outside us' (p. 195). Gross inequalities would be eliminated, he believes, as a consequence of people's independent and critical thought through democratic and progressive education. Shor believes that progressive education is empowering and calls it a 'critical paradigm' (p. 200). It involves a more democratic interaction between students and teachers than is found in the traditional classroom. He refers to the 'third idiom' (p. 260), which, he says, 'is an alternative form of communications for learning, the dialogic model as a whole is a counter-structure to traditional education'.

Dialogue between classroom participants is therefore an essential factor in progressive education, which naturally has implications for the role of the teacher, which is discussed further below. Dewey (1938) believes that educational material should be rooted in the students' own experience. Critical appraisal of this, however, can only transpire through discussion with others. Dialogue is, therefore, important in that it creates a network or community of learners. As Matthews (2005, p. 101) points out, 'Collaboration brings the individual student voice into contact with the voices of others through dialogue'. This gives students the opportunity to articulate and critically analyse their assumptions. Dialogue also involves listening to others' perspectives and thus encourages an openness of mind (Cranton, 2002). It allows students a voice, which is inherently empowering. Overall, this type of learning is student-centred and emerges from, and is intrinsically connected to, experience. According to Rogers (1961, p. 260), this is of utmost importance as 'anything that can be taught to another is relatively inconsequential'.

Woven into the fabric of progressive pedagogy is a feminist perspective that recognises and acknowledges the personal as the political. As exemplified in service-learning, this involves experience and the affective dimension of learning. Taylor (2001) believes that feelings are an important aspect of the learning process and that they are interdependent with cognitive dimensions of learning. There are both positive and negative aspects of this dimension, however, as students may experience discomfort during the experiential learning process, but by discussing this and other personal experiences within small group tutorials allows trust and friendships to emerge. It is this process that can release the power of a learning community and nurture the process of deep learning. A learning community or a small tutorial group may provide an invaluable supportive network. This has been referred to by service-learning students as 'a wee counselling group' (Deeley, 2010, p. 48) which can spur deep learning. Small tutorial groups can become what Southern (2007, p. 335) describes as 'communities of care that support the discovery of self through meaningful relationships, mutual understanding, and collaborative action'.

It is clear that progressive education differs vastly from traditional pedagogy because it involves a holistic approach to learning through cognitive, conative, and affective dimensions. It is potentially powerful and can have transformative effects. This is analogous with Peters (1967, p. 8) who believes that 'to be educated is not to have arrived; it is to travel with a different view', implying that learning is a lifelong activity that provides an enriched outlook. Progressive pedagogy involves generating and developing understanding through meaningful experience. Communication with others is vital for exploring various perspectives, questioning assumptions, and sharing a supportive network. The result can be independent and critical thinkers.

Service-learning easily incorporates these factors within a democratic classroom. A democratic classroom, however, requires a democratic approach by the teacher.

The role of the teacher

In 'traditional' education, power resides with the teacher and students are passive recipients in their acquisition of facts and in their role within the learning and teaching relationship. By contrast, a more democratic classroom is indicative of progressive education where power is shared more equitably (Matthews, 2005, p. 99). Theoretically, this allows for students' intellectual development as they make their own discoveries and construct meaning through their own experience. Despite attempts to create a democratic classroom, a power relationship between the teacher and students cannot be eradicated where the teacher is responsible for the curriculum and factors such as educational aims, intended learning outcomes, and assessment. It may not be possible to achieve a truly democratic classroom, which is a salient and problematic issue with regard to assessment (Deeley, 2014). This is discussed further in Chapter 7. The boundaries of a teacher's role are often imposed and shaped by the expectations of others. It is a socially constructed situation which can be difficult to alter. Indeed, perhaps erasure of power should not actually be contemplated by teachers, but instead, harnessing and utilising their power may be more beneficial and realistic. Denying that power exists in the classroom is not fruitful and the teacher's acknowledgement of power is preferable because it is authentic (Brookfield, 2013). hooks (2009, p. 140) sheds light on this conceptual shift when she describes how she 'began to understand that power was not itself negative. It depended what one did with it. It was up to me to create ways within my professional power constructively'. Through the power bestowed on or inherited by the teacher, then, a type of classroom can be created that emulates a democracy as closely as possible, whereby learner empowerment and students' 'critical becoming' are the ultimate aims. 'The goal of pedagogy', claims Spring (1975, p. 49), 'should be self-development-in the sense of an individual gaining self-awareness and the ability to act', which applies appropriately to service-learning. A classroom which is more democratic than autocratic is a suitable environment to nurture students' empowerment.

There are various implications of an increase in shared responsibility for learning in the classroom. One of the most salient is the teacher's perspective, which, ironically, denotes his or her power per se. If students are to become empowered then it is important that their views are validated (Brookfield, 1998, p. 285). Empowerment of students, therefore, means that the teacher must share his or her power and cast off the mantle of authoritarianism and role of expert in exchange for that of non-directive facilitator, who is capable of metaphorically stepping back to allow room for students' self-directed learning. To do this, the teacher must be confident in his or her role and authentic in the relationship with the students. As Heidegger (1968, p. 15) says, '[T]here is never a place in it for the authority of the know-it-all or the authoritative sway of the official'. The teacher must relinquish the protective barrier of the lecture hall podium, step down from the lecture hall platform to be on the same level as her students, and be prepared to assume a host of different roles (Shor, 1987), which may include that of co-learner (Freire, 1970), mentor, counsellor, and perhaps even 'social worker' (Illeris, 2004, p. 88). A supportive role is particularly salient if a student experiences discomfort in the learning process or undergoes dramatic changes in his or her understanding of the world (Mezirow, 1978).

Progressive pedagogy involves taking a person-centred approach to learning and necessitates the teacher's sharing some power and control with the students. In service-learning, the teacher's position is intrinsically altered when students are on placement, engaged in voluntary work service activities. The teacher has little or no control over the students' service experiences in the community and thus it involves taking risks with regard to what the students learn. Inevitably, this calls for a different approach in the teacher's expectations of students' learning. Rogers and Freiberg (1994, p. 153) offer some insight to this approach by asserting that 'significant learning rests upon certain attitudinal qualities that exist in the personal relationship between the facilitator and the learner'. These qualities include the authenticity of the teacher and his or her capacity for empathy, understanding, and validation of students' experiences and learning. This is the bedrock of trust. Within service-learning, these attributes are absolutely essential to nurturing students' honest critical reflection within the classroom. Hayes and Cuban (1997) discuss the role of the teacher in service-learning, which nestles comfortably within this paradigm of democracy. They refer to service-learning as a 'border pedagogy (which) seeks to transform power relationships and contribute to a more democratic society' (p. 78). It is important to remember that although service-learning provides the environment for this to occur, whether or not it does is dependent on service-learning teachers and their preparedness to share power.

Progressive pedagogy, collaborative learning, and a democratic classroom are all important aspects within a theoretical paradigm for service-learning. Added to this is another fundamental aspect of service-learning, which is experiential learning theory.

Experiential learning theory

Reflecting the polarisation of atomistic and holistic learning as referred to earlier, Bateson (1973, in Brockbank and McGill, 2007) differentiates between models of learning. Firstly, there is the traditional method of teaching and learning dominated by the teacher's authority and power. Knowledge is transferred by and from the teacher to the students, who remain passive recipients. This is at the atomistic end of the learning spectrum. Alternatively, and leaning towards a more holistic approach, there is a model that involves students being aware of their learning and how they learn. Another model of learning, which is firmly grounded in the holistic end of the learning spectrum, involves students' more active participation and interaction with the environment. This latter model includes experiential learning. Experiential learning is holistic in that it involves the whole person in the learning process. Here, there are different areas of learning (Bloom, 1956; 1964, in Brockbank and McGill, 2007). One area is cognitive, which involves the intellectual development of the student. Secondly, there is a conative element, which involves action or developing skills. Thirdly, there is an affective dimension, which involves the role of emotion in learning and personal development. Experiential learning can be defined as 'the sense-making process of active engagement between the inner world of the person and the outer world of the environment' (Beard and Wilson, 2006, p. 19), which indicates a theoretical connection with service-learning. According to Kolb (1993, p. 138), experiential learning gives a 'holistic, integrative perspective of learning that combines experience, perception, cognition, and behaviour.'

Experiential learning is a broad term, however, encompassing various activities. Weil and McGill (1989, p. 4) usefully identify different types of experiential learning, through their 'four village analysis'. The first 'village' involves prior learning, which has not previously been assessed, to be used for accreditation in education at a later period. The second 'village' also involves the value of prior learning to the extent to which it can be built upon and further extended in relation to practical experiences. It is possible that an example of this 'village' might involve continuing professional development for adult learners. A third 'village' that Weil and McGill describe is one wherein experiential learning is 'the basis for group consciousness raising, community action and social change' (p. 12). This is similar to the notion of critical pedagogy, which is explored in the next chapter. Service-learning has a home within this particular 'village', although it also extends along the road to other 'villages'. Finally, a fourth 'village' of experiential learning concerns personal development that emphasises the therapeutic use of past experiences to inform future effective action. These 'villages', or models of experiential learning, are not isolated from one another and are not mutually exclusive.

John Dewey

It is pertinent to take a closer examination of experiential learning through the lens of Dewey's (1933) philosophy of education. He criticises the uncritical reproduction of knowledge and believes that students should learn to solve problems competently, or develop an 'attitude of mind which is conducive to good judgement' (p. 211). Education should nurture independent and critical thinking, and the best way to achieve this, according to Dewey, is through experience. This idea is compatible with the ideas of non-dualism and social constructionism, as discussed earlier. As with learning, Dewey believes that experience can be either active or passive. Similarly, active learning implies motivation and action, whereas passive learning requires little effort. Dewey (1916) explains that learning from experience implies making an active connection between behaviour and its consequences. It is an activity, which is in direct contrast with the traditional model of education, where students are imbued with passivity. Active learning through experience is advocated on the basis of the belief that '[m]ost learning is not the result of instruction. It is rather the result of unhampered participation in a meaningful setting' (Illich, 1971, p. 39). Passivity can lead to boredom and disengagement, which inevitably leads to poor educational performance. Dewey criticises this type of education and advocates a more progressive pedagogy, where the student has opportunities to be actively involved in his or her own learning. Active involvement concerns experience. It is not experience for its own sake because it must be educative, and it is only educative in as far as significant knowledge is acquired. One of the major criticisms of progressive education, however, is that not all experiences are genuinely educative. Dewey admits that experience may indeed be miseducative, for example, if it results in stultification or complacency, lacks meaning, or is in some way detrimental to society. According to Dewey (1916), experience that is educative contributes to our continuous development, which reflects the interaction between us and our environment. He expands this further, saying that 'every experience enacted and undergone modifies the one who acts and undergoes, while this modification affects, whether we wish it or not, the quality of subsequent experiences' (Dewey, 1933, p. 35). This is a core element of service-learning where critical reflection on service experiences and the application of an experiential learning cycle help to inform students' future behaviour. Critical reflection is a vital aspect of an active educative process Dewey describes it as the 'active, persistent, and careful consideration of any belief or supposed form of knowledge in the light of the grounds that support it and the further conclusions to which it tends' (p. 9).

Reflective practice is essential to learning effectively through experience and can lead to informed action. Consequently, critical reflection, which is the focus of Chapter 5, is a key element in service-learning. Reflection concerns recording events and the significant features of experiences. It involves extracting the overall meaning of past events and analysing how this can be synthesised with our current knowledge. Finally, evaluation of events is necessary because this allows our future action to be informed. Dewey explains that firstly, there has to be action, followed by reflection, which is then followed by action informed by reflection until reflection-in-action can be achieved. Schön (1987, p. 311) reiterates Dewey's notion of reflection-in-action whereby there is 'time to shift repeatedly back and forth between reflection on and in action'. Schön explains that this might happen when there is an unexpected result from an otherwise routine action. As a response, reflection on what has occurred can take place and then further action is subsequently influenced or shaped by this reflection. Reflection-in-action occurs in the present and differs from reflection-on-action, which is reflection removed in space and time from action.

Dewey advocates education that nurtures individual growth as a life-long process and one that is manifested through social change to a more democratic community for the common good. In this respect, it is evident that service-learning is heavily influenced by Dewey's philosophical thinking. Similarly, in the ideas of Barnett (1997) and in Freirean pedagogy, there is an aim to nurture individuals' critical thinking, in order to secure a more just society. Dewey (1927) is concerned with the sustainability of democracy through education. There are three strands to this. Firstly, the individual potential capacities of each citizen must be developed and, therefore, the aim of education ought to be moral development. Secondly, education must nurture the active engagement of citizens. Dewey (1916) believes that a 'good society' involves participation and equality through mutually beneficial associations. Thirdly, education ought to promote a humane society and, as such, he advocates the 'freeing of individual capacity in a progressive growth directed at social aims' (p. 98). Overall, this suggests that education should aim to develop individual capacities, but in doing so, it should also be for the benefit of the community. This, in turn, benefits society in general, which sits well within a Communitarian ideological perspective, citizenship education, and service-learning (Annette, 2000b). Community based experience can develop individual capacities, but it can also engage students in active citizenship, which theoretically benefits the individual and the community. This concurs with Stanton's (1990b, p. 186) belief that the 'evolving pedagogy of service-learning is a key to ensuring the development of graduates who will participate in society actively, ethically, and with an informed critical habit of the mind'. Overall, the pedagogy of service-learning is thus positioned appropriately within Dewey's philosophy of education.

Experiential learning cycle

Experience and reflection are two crucially interdependent factors at the heart of the experiential learning cycle. In this cycle, learning is a holistic and fluid process, which involves the environment and the individual's interaction with it. Through this process, experience is reflected upon, interpreted, and transformed into knowledge and understanding. This is an example of non-dualism, where knowledge is not a separate entity from the knower. It is an interrelated process arising from an individual's social interaction with the world.

The various models of experiential learning are remarkably similar. Piaget, for example, believes that 'the dimensions of experience and concept, reflection, and action form the basic continua for the development of adult thought' (in Kolb, 1993, p. 141). Dewey's cycle follows a continuous spiral motion: from impulse to observation, from observation to knowledge, from knowledge to impulse ad infinitum (p. 141). Lewin's cycle begins with concrete experiences, followed by observations and reflections on those experiences. Abstract concepts subsequently arise, followed by the testing of these concepts through new experience (p. 139). What is essentially required in experiential learning, therefore, is direct experience coupled with intentional and critical reflection. According to Kolb (1984), learning is a process that is grounded in experience. It is a continuous phenomenon that requires interaction or transaction, between an individual and the environment, which can result in transformation. Kolb claims it is during the 'interplay between expectation and experience that learning occurs' (p. 28). The experiential learning cycle is fundamental to service-learning both in theory and practice. It is a central factor in its theoretical paradigm and can be used as a structural framework for students' reflective writing.

Adult learning theory

In addition to experiential learning theory, adult learning theory is relevant to a theoretical paradigm for service-learning in higher education. There are various adult learning theories which represent a variety of perspectives concerning adult learning and the ways in which it differs from children's learning. There is an assumption that adults have a wider repertoire of life experience on which to draw, coupled with the effects of age on learning. One of these effects, for example, is to assimilate current knowledge and skills with prior understanding. Knowles (1968, p. 351) differentiates between pedagogy (the learning and teaching of children) and androgogy (the learning and teaching of adults). This is based on the assumption that there is a clear divide between the two, which is problematic when there is no clearly agreed demarcation between childhood and adulthood. Nevertheless, Knowles identifies useful indicators that suggest that learning in adulthood might differ from childhood learning. He explains that adults differ from children in their learning because maturity leads people to use knowledge in a different manner. With a richer variety of past experience, adults tend to assimilate and apply new knowledge whereas children accumulate and store new knowledge for future use. This trend is also associated with the social role of the adult and the use for new knowledge. Life experience may also lead adults to question why and how they learn. Although Knowles's androgogical theory raises awareness of potential differences between adults' and children's learning, it has been met with some reservation and critique. Jarvis (2012b), for example, claims that there is little difference between the learning processes of children and adults. Subsequently, Knowles tentatively retreated from his stance that androgogy is a proven theory and, instead, claims that it provides a framework or basis for developing a theory.

Jarvis (2012a) posits a theory of learning that is applicable mainly to adults, but does not necessarily exclude children and young people. He believes that the level of cognition is likely to be higher with maturity, but claims that all learning arises from experience. The three domains of experiential learning, such as cognitive, conative, and affective, are also relevant in Jarvis's theory. This connects closely with both experiential learning and transformative learning, and, as such, resonates with service-learning. Experiences that cause an element of discomfort are potential sources of learning. This emphasises the role of emotion in learning and the importance of the affective domain (Taylor, 2001). Reason and emotion are claimed to be inextricably linked and interdependent. Taylor explains that 'without the emotional value that gives salience to positive and negative decisions, people are unable to reason' (p. 224).

In adult learning theory, learning involves thought, emotion, action, and experience. One of the main characteristics of adult learning theory is that transformation may occur due to a high level of cognitive development, a deep level of awareness, and a variety of life experience. Adult learning theory, therefore, has similar features to experiential learning. For example, Illeris (2003) believes that there are three dimensions of learning which involve the cognitive, social, and emotional. Here, the cognitive element involves the acquisition of knowledge and skills; the social element concerns interaction within a social context that leads to learning, and the emotional element involves feelings and motivation in the learning process. Jarvis (2006, p. 23) concurs with this tripartite perspective saying that '[a]s individuals are thinking, feeling and acting beings, we transform our experiences through all these dimensions'. Illeris (2004) expounds the adult learning process as involving assimilation, accommodation, and restructuring. Assimilation is knowledge added to what one knows already. Accommodation is accepting new information but first requires some deconstruction or change in understanding or attitude through a process of 'transcendent learning' (p. 84). Restructuring is the result of changes in outlook and behaviour. Altogether, this is transformative learning. Transformative learning often occurs following a critical event, although it can also occur through deep and critical reflection. In service-learning, for example, conditions may arise in students' service in the community that have 'trigger' effects similar to a crisis event (Deeley, 2010, p. 49), although to claim that transformative learning is invariably an inevitable outcome of service-learning is unrealistic. A more feasible claim is that significant and deep learning is highly likely to occur. So, rather than transformation referring to an end state for an individual, it is more reasonable that transformation be perceived as a means to an end, where the end is the actual learning. As Kolb (1984, p. 41) exemplifies, learning is 'the process whereby knowledge is created through the transformation of knowledge. Knowledge results from the combination of grasping and transforming experience'. Whichever interpretation of transformation is applied, it is useful to consider this theory next.

Transformative learning theory

Adult learning theory includes an element of experiential learning theory. It also embraces the notion of change, which might be referred to as 'transformation'. Transformation is not necessarily a characteristic of childhood learning, and, indeed, we may expect changes to occur in children as they are growing up. Moreover, there are various levels of reflection that are apparent in adult learning, which necessitates a level of maturity more commonly found in adults rather than in children and young people (Mezirow, 1978).

The key factors in transformative learning involve experience, critical reflection, and development (Merriam et al., 2007). Emotions are also as vital to transformative learning as experience, critical reflection, and discourse (Taylor, 2001). The factors involved in transformative learning theory are also evident within service-learning. One of these factors is the role of experience which leads to critical enquiry. In service-learning, for example, it is essential that experience is connected to academic coursework, and that students engage in critical reflection on their experiences. Another key factor in transformative learning theory is the role of critical reflection. This allows students the opportunity to consider events which may lead them to question their assumptions. For this process, keeping a diary or journal is recommended (Cranton, 1994).

Transformative learning theory became popular following Mezirow's (1978) initial in-depth analysis and his later theoretical refinements. Further discussion of this is found in Chapter 4. The four main aspects of transformative learning consist of: experience, critical reflection, critical discourse, and action. Interestingly, these are also characteristics of service-learning and, as such, transformative learning theory may sit comfortably within its theoretical paradigm. Experience is gained from students' service to the community; critical reflection and critical discourse on their experience is undertaken in class; and this, theoretically, informs their future action. It is pertinent to note that there is scant 'follow up' research that maps the subsequent action of graduate service-learning students.

Transformation cannot be guaranteed as it depends on the learner and his or her experiences. Transformation, like learning, cannot be enforced, although both can be facilitated. How transformative learning might be facilitated is discussed further in the next chapter. Heidegger (1968, p. 15) shrewdly points out that '[t]eaching is more difficult than learning because what teaching calls for is this: to let learn'. The teacher can facilitate critical discourse and may provide pastoral support for students; however, her role in the theory of transformative learning remains obscure. Nevertheless, the teacher may enhance opportunities for students' learning and their potential transformation by taking a more democratic approach in the classroom, as discussed earlier.

Conclusion

Service-learning is in an advanced state of development in the United States and is developing rapidly and with increasing popularity in the Asia-Pacific region. Lagging behind, service-learning is still in its infancy and remains, so far, generally on the periphery of mainstream, traditional learning and teaching in higher education in Europe and, in particular, the United Kingdom.

The mass of service-learning literature that emerges from the United States suggests that service-learning is beneficial to students and the community in various ways, as outlined in Chapter 1. Within the literature, however, explorations into the undergrowth of meaning or theory of service-learning are limited. This chapter has drawn together various learning theories, ideas, and critical perspectives in order to create a theoretical paradigm for service-learning. This contributes to informed practice of service-learning pedagogy and confirms its capacity for integrity and rigour. If teachers are to employ service-learning to nurture criticality in students or to give students the opportunity to be open to change, indeed, even transformation, it is important that a credulous and robust theoretical basis for service-learning is asserted.

This chapter, therefore, has sought to delineate a theoretical paradigm for service-learning. By examining how thought and language occur and how this affects learning is paramount to understanding how students might construct their internal and external worlds. This paradigm adopts the perspective of personal and social constructionism. Service-learning is also informed by experiential learning theory. Placing service-learning in the context of higher education, it is important to draw on adult learning theory which includes transformative theory, an aspect which is discussed further in Chapter 4.

Within the confines of this theoretical framework lies the notion of progressive education, in particular, collaborative and active learning, the teacher-learner relationship, democracy, and the power structure within the classroom. The power bestowed on the teacher cannot be undone, nor is it being advocated that it ought to be. Rather, the power of the teacher can be utilised to create a more democratic classroom with leadership when it is required for structuring group discussion. The teacher may act as an anchor for students who may experience turbulence in their service-learning, especially if the students' perspectives undergo a seismic shift causing transformation, as discussed in Chapter 4. If service-learning is a pedagogy with the potential for incurring dramatic, or traumatic, effects on or changes in students, then it is an ethical imperative that teachers are prepared to offer support and guidance when needed. Another important role of the teacher is to guide their service-learning students in learning how to think effectively, in particular, how to critically reflect. This aspect is examined in more depth in Chapter 5.

In sum, a theoretical paradigm as explored in this chapter indicates that service-learning is in fact a product of the sum of its parts. Although service-learning is multidisciplinary and a broad umbrella term for a multitude of diverse activities, it is its key components drawing on and being informed by multiple theories that give it a sound coherence. What this means is that the key components of service-learning together contribute to its success as a pedagogy: academic coursework combined with service to the community, which are mutually reinforcing and informing; structured critical reflection on experience shared in small, supportive tutorial groups; and a more democratic classroom where collaborative and active learning occurs and where the teacher-student relationship is reconfigured. Each of these components intersects and connects with different theories and ideas, and so it is asserted that they each contribute to an overall theoretical paradigm for service-learning. The theoretical paradigm, therefore, consists of: experiential learning theory; personal and social constructionism; adult learning theory;

transformative theory; collaborative and active learning theory. In one sense, therefore, it can be said that service-learning is progressive education and is particularly influenced by Dewey. The drawing together and combination of effective processes render service-learning a powerful and rigorous pedagogy. With its emphasis on criticality, democracy, and social justice, however, it is further posited that a theoretical paradigm for service-learning extends to encompass critical theory. In light of this, the aim of the next chapter is to examine service-learning as a critical pedagogy.

4
Service-Learning as a Critical Pedagogy

Introduction

The previous chapter explored various avenues of existing theories populated with the ideas of significant individuals. Ultimately, this led to a theoretical paradigm for service-learning, however, it is not an exhaustive list of potential influences on, or explanations of, service-learning. Indeed, this chapter ventures further afield to embrace an argument for service-learning as a critical pedagogy. Therefore, it proposes that a theoretical paradigm for service-learning may also include critical theory. This perspective resonates with Mitchell (2008) who defines two models of service-learning, that is, the 'traditional' and the 'critical' model. The aim of the latter model is explicitly for social justice, implying that students will actively contribute to social change as a result of participating in service-learning. Taking a critical perspective of this model, however, there is an underlying assumption that students' action for the 'common good' cannot be manifested through the 'traditional' model of service-learning. A problem with differentiating between these two approaches to service-learning suggests that the 'critical' model has an explicit agenda that goes beyond higher educational requirements. For assessment purposes, for example, it would not necessarily be feasible for students to be able to meet the intended learning outcomes of such a model. It could also be argued that a prescribed end goal of social change challenges the idea that service-learning nurtures students' independent thinking. It could be further argued that the model is also based on a specific perspective of justice, namely, a social democratic view of social and redistributive justice with an assumption that students will conform to this particular perspective. This stance disregards the complexities of the contested nature of justice and assumes a shared understanding of 'unjust inequalities'. Service-learning concerns facilitating students' critical thinking processes so that consequently they may act on their critical deliberations. As Barnett (1997) declares, in this way students may ultimately develop into critical beings. Taking a critical perspective of service-learning, it is imperative that its consequences arise spontaneously as a result of students' own independent thinking rather than being prescribed by individual teachers or curricula. A further consideration is also for the future of critical thought and action in that some repressive political regimes may consider the explicit goal of a 'critical' model of service-learning as 'subversive' and therefore ban its introduction into higher education institutions. The view presented in this chapter is that, given the theoretical paradigm outlined in Chapter 3 and with the influence of critical theory in particular, all service-learning is critical. As such, its ultimate aim is for the lifelong development of critical adults. The by-product of this may be social change, but it is not incumbent on, or within the remit of, teachers to impose their views on if, what, and how social change ought to be made. If it were so, then service-learning or any other pedagogy to bring this goal to fruition, ironically, would amount to no more than education as a form of social control. This chapter, therefore, sets out to explore at a deeper level how service-learning may facilitate students' critical awareness, which may, in turn, motivate them to critical action. What that action might be, however, rests upon students' own thinking and not that of the teacher. The teacher's role in service-learning is that of a 'guide' (Chisholm, 2000) and not as a commander.

In order to trace the raising of awareness within service-learning, therefore, critical theory and Freirean pedagogy will be examined as both are relevant to the potential role of service-learning as a social and political process. The process and value of raising awareness through critical thinking will be examined in terms of conscientisation. Drawing on Freire's ideas there is an exploration of this process with examples used from the life of Malcolm X. This is relevant to a discussion of the possible outcomes of critical reflection in service-learning. Following the references made to Mezirow's transformative theory in the previous chapter, further exploration of his theory is relevant in the context of the potential effects of raising awareness and changes that may occur through students' experience of service-learning. To understand service-learning as a critical pedagogy, it is useful to have a preliminary grasp of the basic ideas within critical theory.

Critical theory

With its connections to Dewey, community, and democracy, service-learning can be perceived as a form of citizenship education and, on this basis, there is a role for critical theory within service-learning. Much, of course, depends on the aims and functions of service-learning. If it is agreed, however, that service-learning encompasses examining matters such as civil society, civic virtues, and notions of citizenship, then we are on our way to explaining its rationale as that of contributing to a 'better' society or to the 'common good'.

Historically, in the United Kingdom, the aim of education policy was to tackle Beveridge's metaphorical giant of 'Ignorance'. What students learn and how they learn can serve different interests. Education can serve the interests of the individual, the state, or both. Invariably, one takes precedence over the other, and this largely depends on which political party is in power at any given time and the nature of its education policies. The aim, for example, might be the provision of education in the interests of the individual, although the collective effects of this are that society and the state benefit. Similarly, education can aim to benefit the state, for example, an educated workforce may be beneficial for the national economy, but indirectly individuals will also benefit. Whether the state or the individual is the main beneficiary of citizenship education is questionable. If the state imposes citizenship education on a national curriculum, for example, it could be argued that this represents a 'creeping authoritarianism' (Gifford, 2004, p. 149). In this case, the state might direct what is to be taught in citizenship and how it is to be taught. In this manner, what appears on a citizenship education syllabus can be used as 'a tool for strengthening the supremacy of the State' (Dimitrov and Boyadjieva, 2009, p. 164). In this respect, citizenship education may ultimately concern social control and would be in the interests of the state. Nonetheless, indirectly it may still be in the interests of the individual because with such state control it could be argued that citizens might enjoy a more peaceful society. A counterargument here is that social stability may come at the price of pacification, where citizens are kept in a position of 'semi-intransitive consciousness' (Freire, 2000, p. 48) or under control by being 'bokanovskified' (Huxley, 2005, p. 3). An alternative to this position is that citizenship education can be in the interests of the individual. In this case, citizenship education can be viewed through the lens of personal liberation. By facilitating the process of conscientisation, which is discussed later, citizenship education can offer individuals an opportunity to become critical beings. As such, it can be argued that this is the fundamental position of service-learning and, as such, allows conceptual space for critical theory within its paradigm.

It can be argued that theory is important because it allows meaning to emerge. In service-learning, it is vital that students make sense of their experiences in relation to the theoretical coursework. It can be argued that it is imperative for us to make sense of our experiences, or at least try to do this in our everyday life, whether we are conscious of it or not. We interpret, explain, or predict events in order to understand them. We must also do this in an effort to reach some understanding, or make meaning, of other people's behaviour. Our interpretations, explanations, and predictions are typically based on our own understanding of, or thinking about, the world and how it functions. Our understanding, however, may be flawed and even harmful to ourselves or others. An example of our thinking being harmful to ourselves might be that we do not recognise domestic abuse if it occurs within a close relationship and instead merely accept it as part of the relationship. An example of it being harmful to others is evident in the thinking and understanding of terrorist groups, such as suicide bombers, or individuals such as Anders Behring Breivik, who, on the basis of his personal belief system, killed 77 people in Norway in July 2011. A major problem concerning theory is that sometimes we can uncritically assimilate it from others, especially if it is from whom we perceive as a source of authority. If this happens, and we do acknowledge that it is harming us, we may still mistakenly attribute this harm to our own misunderstandings rather than to a mistaken and harmful theory. Critical theory is highly relevant here because it is concerned with the ways in which we accept the status quo. We might, for example, regard unjust inequalities within society as normal and unchangeable.

Critical theory is concerned with addressing unjust inequalities created by the generally accepted systematic exploitation of the majority of people by a few of the élite. This idea is from a neo-Marxist perspective because it is mainly about interpreting, critiquing, and reformulating ideas from Marxism. The salient concepts within critical theory are unsurprisingly similar to those found in Marxism, such as the notions of false consciousness, hegemony, commodification, objectification, alienation, and praxis. These ideas of critical theory stem from Marcuse, Adorno, and Horkheimer in the Institute of Social Research, Germany, which later became the Frankfurt School of Critical Social Theory.

The concept of false consciousness refers to the belief and acceptance that the way of the world cannot be changed and that it is the natural order of things. In a state of false consciousness or 'semi-intransitive consciousness' (Freire, 2000, p. 48), there is inference of a blind acceptance of one's status, situation, or circumstances in society as being unchangeable. It represents a rigid mindset of uncritical thought, which is reinforced by the prevailing hegemony. Hegemony refers to ideas that are commonly accepted, or taken for granted in society, which appear to be either benign or actively in the interests of the majority of people, whereas they may indeed be harmful. The ideas are prevalent because they are perpetuated by those who benefit from the masses 'buying into' hegemonic ideas, trends, or fashion. Hegemony seeps into every facet of life, from personal relationships to the public realm of community, institutions, and work. Gramsci (1971, p. 350) believes that a hegemonic relationship exists 'throughout society as a whole and for every individual relative to other individuals. It exists between intellectual and non-intellectual sections of the population, between the rulers and ruled, élites and their followers, leaders and led, the vanguard and the body of the army'. Through education, however, hegemony can be identified and challenged. Consequently, critical consciousness can be achieved, which is beneficial to the individual. Moreover, being aware of and opposing hegemony can also involve challenging societal injustices. Through the development of critical consciousness, therefore, not only can there be personal liberation, but also a fairer and just society. What is particularly salient here is that all this can be integral to the aims and functions of service-learning as a form of citizenship education.

The hegemonic process reinforces the notion of commodification whereby the qualities and skills of individuals are reduced to mere products to be hired, bought, or sold on the market. The exchange value of human competencies or endeavours is an inherent part of a dehumanisation process. It is in this process that we become objectified and treated as means to an end rather than ends in ourselves. Subsequently we are alienated from our humanity, reduced, for example, from manual workers to 'factory hands', soldiers to 'boots on the ground', and where potential employees are 'head hunted'. Although these ideas stem from critical theory, they do not stagnate as mere theory or explanations about the world, but are a spur to action in order to make change. Critical action arising from critical thought is referred to as praxis. Ultimately, societal change can emerge from individual or personal liberation. The goal of critical theory, according to Horkheimer (1995, p. 246) 'is man's emancipation from slavery'. This slavery, or oppression, is about being freed from false consciousness. As Davis (1988, p. 22) explains, 'Critical theory...has as its goal the transformation of society, not just the transformation of ideas, but social transformation and thus the reduction and elimination of human misery.'

Becoming aware of the hegemonic influences in our lives is a major breakthrough for the epigenetic growth of critical thinking. Insidiously, these influences can affect and determine our lives, from the way we think and behave, to our personal relationships and expectations. We can become blind under the ubiquitous glare of mass media and marketing ploys where we are guided to believe that the exchange value of commodities, or the price of goods, equates with their intrinsic value. Such materialism is not a modern phenomenon. European 'tulipomania' emerged in the late sixteenth and early seventeenth centuries, for example, when a 'rage for possessing' tulip bulbs that sold at 'preposterous prices' was common (Mackay, 1995, p. 89).

Goods become objects of fetish, incurring in us a desire for them, which produce satisfaction when purchased, often referred to as 'retail therapy'. We can 'buy' into the hegemony and believe that only certain types of goods will satiate our desires. These types of goods are the popular product labels of merchandise which become even more popular when, for example, labels are worn on the outside of garments. This displays to others the wealth or fashion of the wearer to the extent that it obfuscates the fact that it also freely advertises the brand product in the interests of companies' profits.

Similarly, work is also a product. We exchange our physical or intellectual labour for wages. Higher education has become commodified, as a product to be bought and sold. Higher education institutions compete with each other and there are demands to make 'efficiencies' in teaching, such as having large classes. This has a negative impact on progressive pedagogy and experiential learning. A product-profit or market approach to education has negative implications for service-learning in particular, where small classes that enable students' reflective discussions are most effective.

Critical theory also concerns how individuals interpret and understand the world through their personal experience, which resonates with service-learning where students have to make sense of their placement experiences, which are varied and unpredictable. To do this, students must construct and deconstruct their own experiences in order to make sense of them. It involves active, rather than passive, learning. In this sense, education cannot be packaged as a product to be sold at a price. Where critical theory is applied within education, the concept of critical pedagogy emerges.

Critical pedagogy

Critical pedagogy, originating from the ideas and work of Freire, is usually applied to adult education and is more often used when learning and teaching involve critical reflection and transformative learning. The aim of critical pedagogy is ultimately about reinforcing democratic values, such as justice and fairness. It could be argued that this begins in the classroom and is developed through collaborative learning, which resonates with the theoretical paradigm presented in the previous chapter.

Taking the idea that critical theory informs critical pedagogy, such education involves the dissemination of the prevalent ideology in society and the way in which it can be challenged. Inevitably, it involves praxis, or theory and action together, as clearly demonstrated in service-learning. An aim of critical pedagogy is that within education, students must identify the prevailing hegemony. Fromm (1968, p. 153) explains that '[i]deologies are ready made thought commodities spread by the press, the orators, the ideologists in order to manipulate the mass of people for purposes which have nothing to do with the ideology, and are very often exactly the opposite'.

Another aim of critical pedagogy is to recognise sources of power and control. The use of language, for example, is one such source. Politicians and the media press are adept at creating ideas in mass consciousness through the use of phrases and labels. These can then fall into everyday use of language and thus become part of the hegemony. An example of this is the phrase 'weapons of mass destruction' or 'WMD', which was used falsely to justify the invasion of Iraq in 2003. Thinking can be manipulated through language. To soften the news of harsh reality to the masses, carefully crafted warm euphemisms of the 'credit crunch' in 2008, and the later 'double dip recession', sound more like a crispy snack and an ice cream than warnings of an impending wintry bleak economic situation.

Critical pedagogy also concerns challenging the assumptions of the prevailing hegemony and of conventional wisdom or 'common sense'. The mass media is a major source of, or outlet for, hegemonic power and mind manipulation. Through constant and prevailing images in advertising, for example, we are bombarded with particular ideas of what constitutes beauty that become pervasive. This is so powerful that it is not uncommon for women to undergo invasive cosmetic surgery in the pursuit of beauty.

These issues offer fertile resources for close scrutiny in service-learning as part of the basis for critical thinking about sources of power, forms of oppression, and 'false consciousness'. An interesting irony exists, however, whereby social media can be used to counter the hegemonic trends, for example, the underground rapper and hip-hop activist 'Immortal Technique' creates socially conscious music to function as ideology critique. Similarly, citizenship education could be implemented as a government tool of social control, but, ironically, it could also be utilised as a critical pedagogy and function potentially as a tool of revolutionary social reform. Critical pedagogy seeks to raise awareness of power imbalances and develop critical thinking to the point of transforming thought into critical action. This process is referred to as 'conscientisation'. Service-learning offers an ideal opportunity for this to develop.

Conscientisation

The concept of conscientisation is also from the work of Freire and is the English translation of the Brazilian Portuguese word *conscientizaçâo*. The word 'conscientisation' originates from nineteenth-century France, where, as an adjective, it meant 'being conscious'. The word also denoted a noun, which was a 'conscious being'. According to the *Oxford English Dictionary* (1979, p. 846), the word 'conscient' is an adjective meaning 'conscious', although this is now a rare and obsolete form. Interestingly, the adverb 'consciently' remains in usage.

Conscientisation can be perceived as a means to an end and an end in itself. As a means to an end, conscientisation can result in critical consciousness. To achieve critical consciousness involves change: change in ways of thinking and/or ways of knowing. Conscientisation, therefore, can be interpreted as an awakening, an increased awareness, cognition, knowing, or liberation. It can be perceived as an end in itself, which is critical consciousness, and presupposes a high level of intellectual functioning because it is essentially critical.

Freire (1972) believes that conscientisation is a uniquely human process that involves self-awareness of thinking and knowing. We have the capability to detach mentally from our surroundings, which is referred to as being *of* the world (Freire, 1985). As far as we know, other life forms are unable to do this and are constantly in the present, caught in an existence of time always being now. They cannot imagine, plan, or build an abstract alternative. As such, animals are 'a-critical' (Freire, 1972, p. 52) and 'do not elaborate goals; they exist at the level of immersion and are thus a-temporal' (p. 53). Although we have the capacity to detach ourselves from the world, it is also necessary to be immersed in the world for social interactions and relationships, which is referred to as being *in* the world (Freire, 1985). What is significant about human capacity, therefore, is the potential to be *of* the world and conscious of self within the world. Freire (1972, p. 54) draws on Marx (1932, p. 198) to illustrate the essential difference of humans from other life forms, saying that a 'spider conducts operations that resemble those of a weaver, and a bee puts to shame many an architect in the construction of her cells. But what distinguishes the worst architect from the best of bees is this, that the architect raises his structure in imagination before he erects it in reality'.

Despite the human capacity to be of and in the world, some people's thinking may be manipulated and contained within a particular level of consciousness that inhibits critical analysis of their situation. This is a false consciousness which makes them believe that their situation in life is immutable and serves to maintain their subservience to those who are more powerful in society. Drawing on Marxist ideas and the theory of social constructivism, we are socialised throughout life. Language shapes thought so that our understanding is largely a social product. Our beliefs and values, and the stereotypes we may harbour, invariably stem from our earliest experiences, from within the family, or closest nurturing relationships. These ideas, ways of thinking and of seeing the world, invariably influence our current experiences. We may not be aware of these 'frames of reference', or we may be unable to articulate, understand, or change our 'meaning perspectives' (Mezirow, 2009, p. 93). We live, therefore, by sets of assumptions about the world and about ourselves within the world. Given this situation, society, culture, and the media may influence our thinking and manipulate us into creating false identities, fears, and beliefs. Mass media, utilised by either private enterprise or state processes, fan our insecurities for the benefit of powerful individuals, profit, corporations, or governments within the prevailing hegemony. It is, as Mills says (1956, p. 314), 'the formula of a pseudo-world which the media invent and sustain'. This is opposed to, and stultifies, critical thinking. Mills perceives the mass media as a 'malign force ... (which) ... neither enables the individual to transcend his narrow milieu nor (clarifies) its private meaning' (p. 314). It is in the interests of the 'power elite' or the ruling body that such social control is exacted. The metaphorical blindfold on the mass population keeps them from perceiving reality. This results in their oppression, and, subsequently, the public remain in, what Freire (1985, p. 73) describes as, a 'culture of silence'. Bottomore (1971, p. 52) claims that this is indicative of 'the immediate consciousness which workers have of their situation', which refers to false consciousness (Lukács, 1971).

Escape from false consciousness can be through a process of conscientisation, which can be explained as a raising of awareness. Conscientisation can lead through different raised levels of consciousness and, ultimately, to a state of criticality. This process is, however, more complex than a mere awakening. There are, explains Freire (1985), different levels of consciousness to traverse in this process. These are examined here with reference to Malcolm X (1968).

Semi-intransitive consciousness

Being in semi-intransitive consciousness is a state of existence where we are submerged in the world in a state of false consciousness. Here there is neither a possible detachment from the physical world nor tangible divide between it and the world of abstract critical thought. In this state of consciousness, there is no room for a critical view because society and its cultural beliefs are accepted as unquestionable. It is a state of ignorance, where we do not realise that there are, or might be, structural or external reasons for our situation. Trapped in semi-intransitive consciousness, this is merely the way of the world (Congreve, 1971). Consequently, through a lack of awareness, there exists a 'culture of silence' (Freire, 1985, p. 76) where it is impossible for individuals to articulate their oppression. Freire explains that because people lack insight to, and understanding of, the structural forces that shape their life circumstances, they attribute their predicaments to false sources. These sources include self-blame as individuals assume responsibility for their own misfortune or believe that they are unable to change the misfortune that has enveloped and characterised their life. Alternatively, the blame for misfortune or injustice may be projected to 'some superreality' (p. 75) where there is a suggestion of supernatural intervention, which gives rise to people's superstition and fear. Consequently, they may use lucky charms and esoteric rituals in an attempt to ward off evil spirits and to invite benevolent spirits to help them. This level of semi-intransitive consciousness may be perceived, therefore, as a type of 'magical' consciousness, where there is a belief in unknown deities. It is also at this level that organised religion may play a vital role in the lives of the poor and destitute because it gives them hope of a better life, either now or in a perceived after-life. It could be argued that people can be oppressed, not only by the power elite, government, or structures within society (Freire, 1970), but also by trusted and personal connections, such as those within an organised religion or an intimate partner relationship where there is domestic abuse. Indeed, Stark (2007) elaborates articulately on this latter issue, where individuals exercise coercive control over their partners. He refers to this as 'entrapment' (p. 229) and remarks on its similarity to a hostage situation. In a state of false consciousness, oppression can be internalised and may be drawn to the oppressor in a desire to be like him or her (Freire, 1970). An example of this is where Malcolm X (1968, p. 136) describes how he had absorbed a need to identify with white men by having his hair straightened despite the pain and discomfort involved of having a 'conk'. Using lye in the process, he describes how his 'head caught fire. I gritted my teeth and tried to pull the sides of the table together. The comb felt as if it was raking my skin off' (Malcolm X, 1968, p. 137). Later in life, Malcolm commented to others who had had their hair conked, 'Ahhhh, brother, the white devil has taught you to hate yourself so much that you put hot lye in your hair to make it look more like his hair' (p. 29). This reiterates Freire's (1970) theory of oppression when the oppressed seek to identify with their oppressor because they are so deeply imbued with their dominant values.

Semi-intransitive consciousness, however, need not be a permanent state as people can be roused from their false consciousness. Extraordinary events, such as war, earthquakes, tsunamis, or famine, that cause disruption to external environments may also cause internal disturbances and cause disjuncture in thinking processes. An adverse or traumatic life event or situation, such as a serious illness, divorce, or traffic accident, may also cause a hiatus in one's habitual thinking processes. Other motivating events, such as changes in societal structures or pedagogical methods, can also cause subtle changes in perception so that people can gradually move away from a semi-intransitive consciousness to a more analytical perspective where there is awareness of a need for change. These events often incur a change in thinking and behaviour. They are, therefore, pivotal and as such can be referred to as critical incidents. This can lead to the dawning of a different level of thinking, conceptually referred to as 'naïve transitive consciousness' (Freire, 1985, p. 77).

Naïve transitive consciousness

Freire believes that this level of consciousness arises through the cracks and fissures appearing in a lower level of awareness. These gradual openings, possibly created through critical incidents, are the threshold from semi-intransitive to naïve transitive consciousness. They begin in individuals and spread to groups. It is akin to a slow awakening, an emerging and blossoming of increased awareness of hegemonic influences and oppression.

This level of consciousness is characterised by an awareness of negative aspects, influences, and processes in society. These may take the form of, or occur through, covert or overt unfairness, injustice, coercive control, victimisation, discrimination, or oppression. At this level of consciousness, there is a loosening of, but insufficient critical momentum to be able to detach from, these oppressive reins. Consequently, there may be tension between the oppressed and the oppressor, which indicates that a transition is imminent. This might be characterised by a tension in society between what Freire (1985) describes as the power elite and the masses. He says, 'Contradictions come to the surface, provoking conflicts in which the popular consciousness becomes more and more demanding, causing greater and greater alarm on the part of the elites' (p. 78).

This type of situation is not confined to historical accounts of oppressed people. It is also evident in countries where there is democracy as well as where there are dictatorships. An example concerns the current global recession, where the clandestine activities of bankers and stock exchange financiers were gradually disclosed to the public. Another example is the inflated expense claims of members of the British government, which were revealed in the national newspapers in 2009. In this regard, Freire's words are uncannily prophetic as they unearth potential awakenings from semi-intransitive consciousness, '[j]ust as there is a moment of surprise among the masses when they begin to see what they did not see before, there is a corresponding surprise among the elites in power when they find themselves unmasked by the masses' (p. 77). On an individual level, an awakening from a semi-intransitive to a higher level of naïve transitive consciousness can occur. It could be said that in his autobiography, Malcolm X (1968, p. 258) undergoes a similar transition when he reveals the dawning of his acceptance of the ideas of 'The Honourable Elijah Muhammad' saying, 'Not for weeks yet would I deal with the direct, personal application to myself, as a black man, of the truth. It still was like a blinding light'. This was just one of his critical moments, although more were to occur.

Circumstances which afford further insight to internal thoughts and external structures allow a portal to an even higher level of consciousness to be achieved by individuals or, indeed, the mass population. The level is that of critical consciousness.

Critical consciousness

To arrive at a level of critical consciousness, which, according to Freire (1985, p. 86), is 'the maximum of potential consciousness', is a defining moment in overcoming false consciousness. It is an acute awareness and deep understanding, or *verstehen*, of our conditioning. We are conditioned to accept conventional wisdom, or 'common sense', but this largely constitutes hegemonic assumptions which are culturally, socio-politically, or religiously created. For example, the constant and irrepressible bombardment of messages from the mass media induces a socially constructed reality. The messages contain political and ideological propaganda which may be difficult to avoid and not to internalise, because there is little alternative. This miasmic milieu is all pervasive. It may appear to be harmless or trivial, but it functions against our best interests because the primary concern of hegemony is the interests of, and protects, those in power. This situation can occur in all kinds of society, be it democratic or autocratic. 'The subtlety of hegemony', says Brookfield (2000, p. 138), 'is that over time it becomes deeply embedded, part of the cultural air we breathe'. Dispersing these mystifying clouds is to achieve a level of critical consciousness. This infers that we need to become aware of the influences on our thoughts and beliefs, to rid ourselves of indoctrination and other obstacles that have previously obfuscated our perception. We may then finally enter a 'demythologized reality' (Freire, 1985, p. 85) which is removed from oppressive and de-humanising structures. Critical consciousness, however, cannot arise from inertia. It is a state of activity, or praxis, where critical action is informed by critical thought.

As stated earlier, conscientisation can be regarded as an end goal in that it represents critical consciousness. It is also a process in that conscientisation involves a progression through the stages of awakening, that is, from semi-intransitive to naïve transitive consciousness. Conscientisation, therefore, is an evolving journey through different stages or levels of consciousness to the ultimate achievement which is the attainment of critical consciousness. In one sense this is a journey of no return: we cannot un-know what we know and we cannot fail to understand what we have come to understand. Nevertheless, this does not imply that critical consciousness is forever an end state for anyone. Indeed, critical consciousness is a form of detachment from the world. We must, however, live in the world and we cannot sustain an existence that is purely of the world. To maintain critical consciousness at all times in all places would be impossible. We are social creatures with basic needs that must be met in the world in order to survive. Critical consciousness, therefore, is fluid, as are all levels of consciousness. We constantly move from one level to another in different spheres and in different circumstances, even during sleep. It is part of a lifelong learning process as critical consciousness cannot be sustained consistently. Conscientisation is therefore a continuous act or process of becoming critically conscious. It is at this stage we would be more appropriately described as human 'becomings' (Donnison, 1991, p. 57) where there is no end state.

Critical moments in the process of conscientisation can be identified in Malcolm X's autobiography, which enable him to move between levels of consciousness. At school, his teacher had made assumptions about his future employment on the basis of his skin colour. This, says Malcolm, 'was to become the first major turning point of my life' (Malcolm X, 1968, p. 117). Another critical point occurred with Elijah Muhammad's punishment of Malcolm by silencing him following the media consternation of the latter's comments concerning the news of President Kennedy's assassination in 1963, recorded as 'Black Muslims' Malcolm X: "Chickens Come Home To Roost"' (p. 411). Later, Malcolm experienced another vital turning point during his pilgrimage to Mecca, or hajj, where he realised that whites could share his religious faith. He explained that [t]he Muslims of 'white' complexions who had changed my opinions were men who had shown me that they practiced genuine brotherhood' (p. 468). Critical points offer the chance to shift perspective and make transformative changes.

The value of conscientisation

It could be claimed that conscientisation is a valuable process and ultimately a valuable goal to be achieved, but why is it important to raise our awareness and to strive for critical consciousness? It could be argued that the process of conscientisation is of value because it enhances our humanity. It can contribute to a lifelong development of understanding, wisdom, and becoming more humane. The whole idea of conscientisation is akin to that of awakening. Awakening is valued because it is a form of freedom, dispensing with obscurity and dispersing false illusion. It can increase well-being because it is a form of realisation and subsequently of empowerment. Awakening is a process which initially requires becoming aware or conscious of one's situation. Secondly, the process involves recognition of how that situation arose. Thirdly, there is acknowledgement that the negative effects of the situation can be overcome. Finally, there is the recognition of a solution to counteract the negative effects through appropriate action. As Fromm (1978) believes, the path to such change is evident in Buddhist philosophy, Marxist analysis, and psychoanalytic processes. The overarching aims of this path are to achieve a sense of well-being; to grow to a mature and contented individual; to be empowered; and to be liberated.

It might be assumed that a process of conscientisation would occur naturally through formal education. As referred to earlier, however, this might not always be the case as the aim of education policy can be primarily in the interests of national efficiency, which mainly benefits the state. In nineteenth-century Britain, for example, the function of education was regarded as a benefit to the state in terms of sustaining the national economy and maintaining social control through socialisation and reinforcement of class divisions. This helped to ensure that the working class would undertake unskilled jobs thus keeping skilled employment for the middle class. Education can tame students and train them to think in particular ways. These ways can be dulled, passive, and lead to dependency in thought. Education systems are often based on achieving quantifiable results through the attainment of grades and scores. This leads to students' strategic learning and the idea that education is a commodity used in order 'to get on' in the world. Currently, mass higher education inevitably forces graduates to compete more aggressively in the labour market. It is not surprising that universities emphasise the need for students to develop their skills and attributes in preparation for the workplace (CBI, 2009) especially in times of economic recession and 'austerity' where the competitive search for employment is 'fierce' (Deeley, 2014, p. 41). In these circumstances, the focus of education can easily slip into a mere strategic acquisition of skills without necessarily an accompanying growth in intellectual and personal development. It is in this context that conscientisation becomes more pertinent.

Barnett (1997) believes that the critical thinking is the crux of higher education but thinking critically does not necessarily come naturally or easily (Peters, 1967). Critical thinking is a skill that must be learned as clearly it does not occur through a process of osmosis. Some of the main difficulties of critical thinking are that it must be pursued continually and that it requires both self awareness and self-surveillance. As a critical thinking skill, critical reflection also requires motivated and committed application. It is through critical reflection that one may determine one's entrapment within societal structures, search for and possibly discover the appropriate keys that unlock the doors to greater understanding. These keys are metaphors for critical points that can occur in the lives of individuals. Keys may not always be used, of course, similarly, critical points may not be recognised as such and, as a result, critical thinking can be stifled.

Although as humans we have the capacity to reflect and thus undergo changes in consciousness to free ourselves (Freire, 1972), we do not always avail ourselves of this course of action. Like bovine animals, the herding instinct is compelling, not unlike following 'tweets', where there is 'safety in numbers', or conforming to the majority trend, as Mills (1956, p. 312) affirms, '[t]o accept opinions in their terms is to gain the good solid feeling of being correct without having to think'.

Dewey (1927, p. 159) claims '[h]abit is the mainspring of human action, and habits are formed for the most part under the influence of the customs of the group'. There is a need for many to conform or follow what they perceive to be the most popular trend, whether it be fashion, a chic 'look', fashionable places 'to be seen', or fashionable words and phrases to use. In attempts to persuade us to buy products, advertising and the mass media manipulate our thinking, reinforcing stereotypes and fuelling our fears of inadequacy. In the 'aporia of mass culture' (Adorno, 2001, p. 85), there exists a 'massified culture industry' (Aronowitz, 1977, p. 768) that subsumes and dominates collective consciousness. From saleable commodities comes a pernicious paradigm of attitudes and thinking. Lukács (1971, p. 84) believes that 'commodity fetishism is a *specific* problem of our age, the age of modern capitalism'. Also problematic is the unperceiving

mind that unquestioningly accepts this, as it is 'pre-organised attitudes and emotions that shape the opinion – life of the person'
(Mills, 1956, p. 313). Herein lies slavery.

The effects of this type of thought control and manipulation are
habit forming. Habitual behaviour may be characterised by unconscious action. Dewey (1927) believes that our habits are influenced
by society and that these affect our behaviour and thinking. The
personal is transmuted to the social and vice versa. He says that
'[h]abits of opinion are the toughest of all habits' (p. 162). The reason
for this is that such habits stifle critical thought. Even if there is
awareness that habits of mind can hinder the raising of consciousness, there may remain a reluctance to acknowledge a critical point
if it occurs and thus miss an opportunity for personal growth.
There is a comfort to be gained in what is habitual and familiar,
and conversely, there may be discomfort, anxiety, even fear, in
what is unfamiliar and unknown. Generally, we do not like change.
Consequently, we may adopt a stance of passive acceptance and life
in a state of slumber. Without the process of raising awareness, or
conscientisation, we are at risk of becoming 'enslaved to the concrete'
(Aronowitz, 1977, p. 769). The implications of this may be understood
in situations where women willingly undergo surgery to alter the size
and shape of their body, and lighten or colour their skin, as a consequence of hegemonic persuasion to conform to what is perceived to
be an acceptable or desirable image. Other persuading pressures also
act to shape our behaviour, or worse, others' behaviour towards us
that is detrimental to our well-being. The perceived transgression of
prescribed codes of conduct, for example, can lead to women's ostra-
cism, shame, and honour-based killings (Sanghera, 2007). Cruel,
unnatural acts, such as female genital mutilation are also performed
in the name of unquestioned hegemonic cultural beliefs (Hirsi Ali,
2008). Religious fundamentalism, traditions, and cultures, can facilitate acritical habits of mind and behaviour. Fromm (1978, p. 42)
concurs, describing any form of religious zeal as, 'a crutch for those
who want to be certain, those who want an answer to life without
daring to search for it themselves'.

The value of conscientisation is that it raises awareness and facil-
itates critical thought. The ability to think critically is imperative
if we wish to initiate personal or social change. Thinking critically
affects our personal ontological and epistemological understandings

of our environment. Critical thinking is crucial to autonomy and authenticity. We have a choice, however, as we can either passively absorb the current hegemony or we can produce our own critical understanding. To do the latter, we must preserve our autonomy, make informed choices, challenge hegemony, and instigate changes in society for the common good and social justice. Inevitably this is political, especially if education is used as a means to personal emancipation and the development of critical beings. This must occur in the areas of knowledge, self and the world and should involve 'critical thinking, critical action and critical self-reflection' (Barnett, 1997, p. 1). There are various pedagogical methods and processes that might achieve this end: service-learning being one.

In sum, conscientisation is vital because it concerns raising awareness and developing consciousness. It allows a more critical perception that serves to challenge propaganda and the 'mystification of reality' as the 'dominant classes...obscure the real world' (Freire, 1985, pp. 115–16). If critical consciousness does not occur at any level then political illiteracy and oppression will fill the void. Critical thinking is the antidote to the cultural creation of mass dullness. Conscientisation is the tool for emancipation from social control, oppression and endemic hegemonic influences. Critical thinking and critical reflection can lead to conscientisation, which subsequently can lead to personal and societal transformation. All these factors can intersect seamlessly through service-learning, affirming the assertion that is a critical pedagogy.

Transformative learning theory

Transformative learning theory was referred to in Chapter 3 as being part of a theoretical paradigm for service-learning. It is pertinent to revisit this in the context of critical pedagogy and conscientisation. Education is often seen as a process or result of change. Change can be in various and interconnected forms, such as knowledge and skills or attitudes and behaviour. Not all change is transformative and not all education is transformative. It would be unrealistic and perhaps to some extent unethical to aim for transformation, because it cannot be forced and it may also be interpreted as paternalism, indoctrination, or control. Transformation can be the result of liberation from oppression. In this sense, liberation is personal.

Either as teachers or revolutionaries, we can only help to facilitate another's liberation.

Transformation can occur through education. Indeed, Mezirow (1994, p. 226) believes that '[t]ransformative learning is central to what adult education is all about'. It is posited that service-learning in higher education is conducive to transformation, but to understand this, we must first understand what is meant by transformation. Mezirow (1981, p. 11) claims that we each make our own sense of the world and our experiences within it, saying that '[a]wareness of *why* we attach the meanings we do to reality, especially to our roles and relationships–meanings often misconstrued out of the uncritically assimilated half-truths of conventional wisdom and power relationships assumed as fixed-may be the most significant distinguishing characteristics of adult learning'.

In the social construction of our own reality, there are two vital factors needed for making meaning. These factors are our frames of reference, or what might be considered rules and principles. It is important that we have meaning in order to understand. In this sense, 'meaning' is our interpretation and begins in our very early, indeed pre-linguistic, development in babyhood. It is our frames of reference that guide our learning and memory. Frames of reference include 'meaning perspectives' and 'meaning schemes' (Mezirow, 1990, p. 2). Meaning perspectives are the product of socialisation and include, for example, our acquisition of language. Meaning perspectives can be seen as habits of mind or expectation which help us to interpret and make sense of our experience. Mezirow believes that '[b]ecause we are all trapped by our own meaning perspectives, we can never really make interpretations of our experience free of bias' (p. 10). He explains that there are three types of meaning perspectives, one of which is epistemic. This concerns what we know, the way we know it, and how we use knowledge. A second type of meaning perspective is sociolinguistic and concerns how our language is used in a social context. A third type of meaning perspective is psychological, which concerns what we understand to be our self and what are our needs and preferences. Each of these types of meaning perspective has several meaning schemes through which our habits of mind are expressed. Meaning schemes include knowledge, values, and beliefs which guide our expectations and behaviour. These can be changed more easily than meaning perspectives, which are the bedrock of who we understand ourselves to be. Meaning perspectives are thus very difficult to change, as Mezirow (1991, p. 202) affirms, saying that '[p]erspective transformation is a mode of adult learning that neither learner nor educator is able to anticipate or evoke upon demand'. From this explanation taken from Mezirow's transformative learning theory, it is apparent that there it fits within the theoretical paradigm for service-learning expounded in the previous chapter.

Transformative learning can occur through changes to our frames of reference. These changes may be facilitated through various means, either incidental or deliberate. Incidental facilitation of change can also occur naturally through life experiences, such as illness or bereavement. Mezirow (1991, p. 193) describes the source that can effect change as a 'disorienting dilemma'. Deliberate facilitation of change could also be through critical reflection or challenging assumptions. As Mezirow clearly states, 'Any major challenge to an established perspective can result in a transformation. These challenges are painful; they often call into question deeply held personal values and threaten our very sense of self' (p. 168). Deliberate attempts to induce transformative change in students through education incur risk and, in so doing, teachers must acknowledge an ethical responsibility. Transformative change may occur unintentionally in service-learning, as discussed here.

Service-learning

Service-learning can provide an ideal pedagogical environment for transformation to occur as there is a similar process of reflection and action that is necessary within transformative learning theory. Mirroring the experiential learning cycle used in service-learning, Mezirow (1994, pp. 222–3) states that '[l]earning is defined as the social process of construing and appropriating a new or revised interpretation of the meaning of one's experience as a guide to action'. His idea of the transformative process mirrors the experiential learning cycle, saying that one should become 'critically reflective of one's own assumptions as well as those of others, engage fully and freely in discourse to validate one's beliefs, and effectively take reflective action to implement them' (Mezirow, 2000, p. 25). Transformation cannot occur solely through the transmission of knowledge (Grabove, 1997), however, it can occur through particular teaching and learning strategies (Cranton, 1994). These strategies can include experiential learning, challenging assumptions (Belenky and Stanton, 2000), raising awareness, and through writing reflective journals and critical incidents. All of these factors are found within service-learning.

Much of the basis for our understanding stems from our assumptions and what we take for granted as true. Paradigmatic assumptions are those that concern our values and beliefs and provide the parameters of our identity. Prescriptive assumptions are grounded in social, cultural, religious, or political ideology. These assumptions concern, for example, what constitutes socially acceptable behaviour or a 'good society'. Causal assumptions concern what we consider to be the causes of external events in the world. 'Questioning assumptions', warns Brookfield (1990, p. 178), is 'psychologically explosive ... (and) educators who foster transformative learning are rather like psychological and cultural demolition experts'. Mezirow (1991, p. 168) agrees that '[t]hese challenges are painful; they often call into question deeply held personal values and threaten our very sense of self'.

Service-learning 'experiences often create dissonance, doubt, and confusion' (Bringle and Hatcher, 1999, p. 181), which can challenge students' 'frames of reference' (Mezirow, 2009, p. 92). Rogers (1969, p. 159) asserts that if there are challenges or contradictions to one's inner self, then '[a]ny learning which arises from this dilemma is painful and threatening ... any learning which emerges from the contradiction involves a definite change in the structure of self'. He adds that 'all significant learning is to some degree painful and involves turbulence' (p. 339). Shor (1987, p. 107) reinforces this, suggesting that the teacher may be in a position where she is metaphorically 'an exorcist confronting a panoply of dybbuks'. It is important for learners to be made aware of the possible consequences of embarking on this path of self-awareness. This responsibility is a moral one and it lies with the teacher to fully inform her students of the potential effects that might occur and to provide pastoral support for them should it be needed. It is vital to raise awareness of the potentially distressing effects of challenging assumptions in the process of critical reflection. As such, it is imperative that 'students should be taught to disengage with reflection' (Bulpitt and Martin, 2005, p. 213) which may be difficult, as Romeo testifies, 'O, teach me how I should forget to think!' (Shakespeare, 1967, p. 63).

A helpful factor in this process is the creation of a supportive learning environment that can be created through service-learning. This is exemplified by Boyd and Myers (1988, p. 10) who believe that 'learning is a social process and discourse becomes central to making meaning' and therefore small groups, or 'learning communities', are ideal contexts within which transformative learning can be nurtured. It is the quality of such groups, where trust is essential, that enhances the transformative process (Wilhelmson, 2002; Mezirow, 2000). Within such an environment, students can learn from and support each another (McAlpine, 2004; Jacques, 2000; Mezirow, 1991). This is pertinent to service-learning, where the safe sharing of experiences can enhance students' understanding through critical reflection and discourse. This view is reinforced by Brockbank and McGill (1998, p. 197), who say that, 'when students experience empathy, they recognise the power of an understanding response that builds trust, establishing the basis for a relationship within which it is safe to engage in reflective dialogue, and thus enables critically reflective learning'. Indeed, what can also transpire is transformation, or at least some degree of change. It is this change at a personal level that may ultimately affect societal change when students' critical thinking transmutes into their critical action or praxis. Surely, it is then that service-learning may truly be considered a critical pedagogy.

Empirical evidence

As demonstrated in Chapter 2, there is evidence that service-learning affects students in different ways. In a research study for a MEd in Academic Practice (Deeley, 2007), students were found to reveal personal change that they had experienced during a service-learning course. Selections from these data are presented here.

The findings in this study largely reiterated explanations of transformative change described in the literature (Rogers, 1969; Brookfield, 1990; Mezirow, 1991, 2000; Cranton, 1994). All the students claimed that the course had changed them. For some, the change was gradual, but for others it was a sudden transformation (Deeley, 2010; Wilhelmson, 2002). The students' accelerated personal development and increased intellectual development were interrelated because they stemmed from the same causes. These included the challenges brought by engaging in critical reflection, examining assumptions, and being on placement. One student explained, '[T]he things that you've taken for granted and not really thought about start to get challenged'. Another student affirmed this, saying, '[W]e're challenging ourselves. That's a really personal thing'. For some, it was a matter of facing their 'own demons as well' (Deeley, 2010, p. 49). Discomfort, dissonance, and negative emotions were all evident, but they transmuted into positive factors because they led to valuable learning. Subsequently, a student mirthfully recommended putting a health warning on the service-learning course.

One student wrote authentically about her service-learning experience, saying that it 'led me not only to change myself, but to change my perception of the world around me – to be less in the world and more of the world. Such transformation is difficult and often painful, but it is transformation I feel to be worthy and true and one which has made me a better person'. Challenging their own attitudes, rather than taking them for granted, became a frequent issue of revelation for the students. The result of this was that they did not 'jump to conclusions' about other people quite as readily as they had done prior to the course. Most of the changes had positive effects, such as having a more mature outlook and being 'more open minded...doing things I wouldn't have done before'.

Another student admitted that 'I'm trying to change, even just small things in my own life and that's how much this course is affecting me'. She explained this as 'changing the way I think or understanding the way I think, understanding how I feel about situations, of how I act in situations'. The effects of the course were that some students began to perceive and challenge oppression in their life. It is imperative, however, to retain a critical perspective of service-learning and what this pedagogical approach potentially can achieve. Poignantly, transformative personal or societal changes cannot be predicted or guaranteed.

Conclusion

This chapter has extended the theoretical paradigm of service-learning as presented in Chapter 3, by explaining how service-learning can be regarded as a critical pedagogy. Freirean critical pedagogy is informed and underpinned by critical theory, so an exploration of this and why it is relevant in the context of service-learning was explored. For service-learning to instigate students' critical thinking and critical action, or praxis, in order to instigate and secure social justice for a better society which would serve the common good, it is imperative that students engage in consciousness raising. Explaining Freire's (1985) concept of conscientizaçâo or conscientisation as a means to an end as well as an end in itself, this chapter outlined the different levels or stages involved and their effects. These levels are referred to as semi-intransitive, naïve transitive, and critical consciousness. Examples from the autobiography of Malcolm X were highlighted to illustrate critical incidents that can initiate transference and progression from one level of consciousness to another. Such examples as these, extracted from influential individuals, real life incidents, and literature can be powerful and stimulating resources for, and that resonate with, service-learning students. The intrinsic value, purpose, and effects of conscientisation were then outlined. The impact of this process is compatible with Mezirow's transformative learning theory. Although this was referred to in Chapter 3 as part of the theoretical paradigm for service-learning, it is in this particular context of service-learning as a critical pedagogy that conscientisation is more clearly apparent. Some selected findings from a research study, undertaken for a dissertation as part of a MEd. in Academic Practice, were presented to demonstrate the effects of service-learning on students in terms of its transformative potential.

As part of the process of conscientisation and as an essential factor within the pedagogy of service-learning, critical reflection is pivotal. This is examined in the next chapter.

5
Critical Reflection

Introduction

In the previous chapter, service-learning was considered as a critical pedagogy. Part of this assertion involved the imperative of raising awareness through the conceptual Freirean levels of consciousness. Intrinsic to, and impelling this process, is critical reflection. It is critical reflection that plays a vital role in the process of conscientisation and, therefore, contributes to the notion that service learning may be perceived as a critical pedagogy with the potential to effect personal transformation and social change. This chapter, therefore, aims to explore the concept of critical reflection.

Critical reflection is a vital skill for students, enabling them to connect their practical service experiences in the community with their academic coursework. As Boud (2001, p. 10) explains, 'Reflection has been described as a process of turning experience into learning, that is, a way of exploring experience in order to learn new things from it'. As critical reflection is an aspect of critical thinking (Brookfield, 1987), it is inherently part of the metacognitive skills acquisition and development in higher education. It cannot be assumed, however, that students develop these skills spontaneously or naturally, as if through an intrinsic process. Indeed, it has been said that 'the gift of reason and critical reflection is not of man's outstanding peculiarities, and even where it exists it proves to be wavering and inconstant' (Jung, 2002, p. 2). Not surprisingly, it is regarded as necessary to instruct, guide, and facilitate students in their critical reflection (Russell, 2005; Meyers, 1986). To understand this particular thinking process, it is useful to have a clear view of the meaning of critical reflection. As with critical thinking, searching for a definition is an onerous task (Halonen, 1995) because there is no singularly agreed definition of critical reflection and, therefore, its meaning is often based on presumptions. Drawing on the work of John Dewey, this chapter presents a preliminary examination of thinking. This provides a context for, and leads to, a scrutiny of critical reflection. Following an understanding of critical reflection and its value, this chapter then considers how it can be facilitated. This is particularly relevant in service-learning because critical reflection is central to how students connect their service to their academic coursework. In particular, critical reflective thinking skills may be developed through students' writing of critical incidents. This is explored in more depth and with specific examples in Chapter 6 on academic writing in service-learning.

The potential outcomes of engagement with critical reflection on the intellectual and personal development of students will also be explored in this chapter. It is asserted that critical reflection, which connects theory with practice, can deepen students' learning. It can raise their awareness of social and political issues, with the potential of motivating them to engage in praxis, or informed critical action for social justice, as the result of a process of their conscientisation. Finally, the essential factor of critical reflection in service-learning is examined from various critical perspectives, including a focus on the teacher's role.

Thinking

As critical reflection is a form of critical thinking, it is useful to examine what is meant by thinking. Further insight can also be gained by examining the meaning of reflection as a certain type of thought process. Furthermore, an exploration of the notion of criticality is essential to an understanding of critical reflection. These factors are examined here.

What is thinking? As an educational philosopher, it was appropriate that Dewey (1933) posed this question because it is at the root of our understanding and the process from which we gain meaning in and from the world. Indeed, there are many ways of thinking and forms of thought. One way of thinking about thinking is quite simply to divide it between the concrete and the abstract. Both are tools: concrete thought, for example, aids our survival. It is the type of thought that helps us to solve problems and has a practical use. Concrete thought, therefore, is used as a means to an end. Abstract thought, however, is a form of consciousness that enables us to extend our thinking. It is manifested in our being of the world, rather than our being in the world. According to Freire (1970), abstract thinking divides us from the animal kingdom. It is a 'higher' form of consciousness that allows us to imagine, plan ahead, or foresee the potential consequences of our actions. This resonates with the ideas of Marx and Engels (1970) that our consciousness, like language, exists and develops to facilitate our communication with others.

The concrete and the abstract, however, are not necessarily mutually exclusive. If, for example, we are faced with a very difficult problem which cannot be solved by concrete thinking, we might engage in abstract thinking in order to imagine alternative solutions. In a situation of extreme stress, for example, one that involves our survival, this approach in thinking is likely to occur instantaneously and automatically. A pilot losing control of an aeroplane in flight, for example, might find a way in which to regain control of the aeroplane by thinking in both concrete and abstract terms together to avoid an impending catastrophe.

In Buddhist philosophy, it is believed that thought consists of a stream of consciousness. This consciousness can be of varying random or connected thoughts arising and passing away. The rapidity and fluidity of this process may be perceived by the thinker as continuous thinking, whereas from a Buddhist perspective it is considered to be a series of thoughts (Nārada, 1975). This is similar to an electric light bulb that has a series of on-off vibrations but gives the appearance of continuous light. Consciousness involves thought. As there are different thought forms, there are also different forms or levels of consciousness, as discussed in the previous chapter.

Critical reflection is not an easy or simple task. Gelter (2003) explains that there is an almost incredible amount of information bombarding us through our senses at any given time. In order to comprehend these constant stimuli, our brains exercise a series of filtering mechanisms. He states that in the human brain 'a thousand billion nerve cells reduces in half a second 11 million bits of sensory information to 50 bits of consciousness' (p. 340). Essentially, our subconscious brain activity aids our survival.

Thinking helps us to make meaning of our world. Peirce (in Habermas, 1987) explains a process of inferential thinking that contributes to our understanding. This consists of three forms: deduction, induction, and abduction. Deduction concerns proof and can lead to expectation of a specific outcome. Induction involves our expectations of specific outcomes and whether these expectations can be validated and confirmed. Finally, abduction is a form of hypothesising and refers to thinking that a certain outcome will occur. Thought, therefore, is aligned to our beliefs. Reflective thought is, according to Dewey (1933, p. 9), '[a]ctive, persistent, and careful consideration of any belief or supposed form of knowledge in the light of the grounds that support it and the further conclusions to which it tends'.

Critical reflection

In an attempt to define critical reflection, it is useful to begin with the concept of reflection. Although it is frequently used synonymously with critical reflection, fundamentally, reflection can be perceived as merely looking back on events or experiences. It implies recall and memory, or images of the past. The purpose of reflection may be similar to critical reflection in that it may be intended to lead to a greater understanding or awareness. As Mezirow (1998, p. 186) clarifies, 'Reflection does not necessarily imply making an assessment of what is being reflected upon, a distinction that differentiates it from critical reflection'. By contrast, '[r]eflection on presuppositions is what we mean by *critical reflection*' (Mezirow, 1990, p. 6).

Reflection is a process and a product. The process is the act of making meaning and its product is the meaning itself. In order to make the process of reflection effective, it is valuable to know what the process entails. Reflection is bringing into consciousness that which may be unconscious or half forgotten. Boud et al. (1985) refer to Mezirow's seven stages of reflectivity, from first becoming aware to perspective change. Similarly, King and Kitchener (1994) illuminate seven stages of reflective thinking. The first three stages are characterised by pre-reflective thinking where there is no evidence of questioning knowledge. This stage is not dissimilar to Freire's concept of semi-intransitive consciousness. Stages four and five of King and Kitchener's seven stages are regarded as quasi-reflective thinking. Here there is an awareness of the uncertainty of knowledge, but there is a deficit in knowing how to progress, similar to Freire's naïve transitive level of consciousness. According to King and Kitchener, reflective thinking is achieved in stages six and seven, where assumptions are acknowledged, challenged, and new meanings can emerge. Parallel to this stage is Freire's idea of critical consciousness.

Critical reflection could be described as an act of purposeful inquiry. It is construed as 'principled thinking; ideally, it is impartial, consistent, and non-arbitrary' (Mezirow, 1998, p. 186). Dewey (1933, p. 3) describes it as 'the kind of thinking that consists in turning a subject over in the mind and giving it serious and consecutive consideration'. An interesting insight to reflective thinking is offered by Rotenstreich (1985) who explains that reflection is a matter of considering how we think, what we think, and what leads us to believe that our thoughts are accurate and real, or the extent to which they are valid.

The acts of identifying and challenging assumptions are a necessary part of critical reflection. As Barnett (1997, p. 91) claims, 'In critiquing one's present understandings, new understandings can emerge'. The aim, therefore, is to make meaning. Assumptions may be personal, belonging to other people or to society in general. Understanding how assumptions are made may alleviate the difficult process of change, particularly if alternative ways of thinking or action are also considered. Challenging our assumptions can be disorienting and give way to feelings of discomfort. This reinforces Brookfield's (1987, p. 7) view that '[c]ritical thinking is emotive as well as rational'. Critical reflection, therefore, may also involve critical self-reflection and be part of a lifelong process of self-development. Reinforcing this perspective, Barnett (1997) believes that for the development of critical beings, reflection is essential to critical thinking and critical action. Critical reflection can result in change, which may bring uncertainty accompanied by discomfort. For service-learning students engaged in critical reflection, this can spur their reluctance to change. Ultimately, this can lead to resistance and rejection of this pedagogy. By contrast, change may be illuminating and transformative 'whenever assumptions or premises are found to be distorting, inauthentic, or otherwise invalid' (Mezirow, 1991, p. 6).

Critical reflection can be instigated naturally or deliberately. For example, natural life events, such as childbirth or bereavement, can stimulate critical reflection on one's assumptions. Other life events may also do the same, such as a divorce, a life-threatening illness, or a serious accident. Critical reflection may also be deliberately exercised without these particular tipping points. It can be utilised as a 'conscious and intentional exploration process leading to a better understanding of complex ideas' (Arcand et al., 2007, p. 17). Critical reflection is, therefore, an appropriate intellectual skill to be developed in higher education, as indeed Dawson (2003, p. 38) claims that it is 'a central concept in adult education'. It is a tool effectively used in conjunction with practical experience. In this sense, critical reflection is a salient feature of experiential learning and, in particular, of service-learning.

Concentration and a focusing of the mind are essential features of critical reflection. As in some Buddhist meditative practices, it is an exercise in directing and maintaining one's attention to a particular object. It involves both a level of consciousness and the awareness of an object. It is a deliberate 'return of consciousness upon itself' (Hodgson, 1878, p. 361). Contrary to a misguided view that critical reflection is synonymous with mindless 'navel gazing', critical reflective practice requires an inordinate amount of energy, time, and quiet space. It can occur 'only when one is willing to endure suspense and to undergo the trouble of searching' (Dewey, 1933, p. 16). As Dawson (2003, p. 38) affirms, '[C]ritical reflection...takes time, space, patience, discipline, and close listening to engage in meaningfully'. It is clear that critical reflection is an activity that requires diligence and focus. The value of quiet contemplation and its facilitative effects on deep learning is explained as 'interiority (which) is about developing spaciousness within us' (Hart, 2008, p. 235). This process can be challenging because it contrasts sharply with current expectations of us to be available for social interaction immediately and constantly through media networks. Ironically, such ubiquitous demands on our attention may produce endemic 'continuous partial attention' (p. 239) and 'surface perception in people (creating) shallow habits of mind' (Shor, 1987, p. 64).

Models of reflection

Typically, most reflective models have a similar pattern consisting of a descriptive element and analytical reflection. This is subsequently followed by attempts to seek meaning by reviewing the original descriptive element through different lenses. Brookfield (1987, pp. 26–27) identifies signposts in reflection as 'trigger events', 'appraisal', 'exploration', 'developing alternative perspectives', and 'integration'. Similarly, Kreber (2004) demonstrates how a model of reflective practice can be used within the scholarship of teaching which involves reflecting on content, problems, actual responses, potential responses, and ultimately on alternative perspectives. Essentially, the process of critical reflection is cyclical and mirrors experiential learning cycles, where concrete experiences occur first and are followed by abstract thinking, as referred to in Chapter 3.

Kitchener and King (1990) outline a model of reflection which takes in to consideration how assumptions and perceptions of knowledge are applied or rejected and modified at different levels of critical thinking. Van Manen (1977) also refers to different levels and functions of reflective thinking. Technical reflection, for example, involves thinking about specific skills, technical knowledge, and its practical application. Contextual reflection concerns investigating assumptions, and dialectical reflection encompasses the abstract theorising of social, political, and ethical matters.

Although various models or methods are used in the process of critical reflection, the essential processes are similar. In service-learning, therefore, the effects of critical reflection may not be guaranteed or, indeed, may differ from what is anticipated. Risk is intrinsic to this process and is a major reason why a supportive learning environment is essential to this form of experiential learning, which is discussed here.

Facilitating critical reflection

Intention

It is important to deliberately encourage students in higher education to develop their critical thinking skills (Halonen, 1995). In particular, critical reflection is vital to service-learning, and therefore it is essential that the development of such skills is facilitated. As stated earlier, it may be assumed that critical reflective skills are inherent and, as a result, it has been claimed that there is a 'lack of explicit strategies and support' (Russell, 2005, p. 203) for critical reflection in the higher education classroom. Nevertheless, there are resources available for the discerning teacher (Ash and Clayton, 2009; Moon, 2006).

It is asserted that the traditional 'banking' style of education is a hindrance to the development of students' critical thought (Meyers, 1986; Freire, 1970; Dewey, 1938). In this passive type of learning, it could be argued that the focus is on accumulating information, rather than developing independent thinking that nurtures intellectual curiosity and growth. Conversely, it could be argued that the process of 'progressive' or experiential education is more conducive to critical thinking. Indeed, in service-learning there is an intention for students to become critical thinkers through critical reflection on their service to the community and their academic coursework. Critical thinking concerns the ability to consider alternative ways of understanding. It is 'not a dispassionate learning process' and can even amount to 'a threatening encounter that challenges one's very "selfhood"' (Meyers, 1986, p. 96). Critical reflection, therefore, may have a personal impact. 'Teaching critical thinking', claims Meyers, 'involves intentionally creating an atmosphere of disequilibrium, so that students can change, rework, or reconstruct their thinking processes' (p. 14). In service-learning, disequilibrium may occur spontaneously as students encounter ill-structured challenges on placement outside the security of organised classes. Student support should be afforded by the teacher, which could take the form of guidance in critical reflection. This might involve, for example, students learning how to structure their thinking, suspend judgement, and develop awareness of how and what they learn. It is incumbent on teachers to facilitate their students' critical reflection as a deliberate and purposeful task.

Stages of critical reflection

Before facilitating critical reflection, it is useful for the learner to be made aware of its different stages, phases or levels. Dewey (1933) analyses the process of reflective thinking that may begin with a dilemma. He says that reflection 'originates in a problem' (p. 281). In this case, a situation may arise that causes the student to stop in her tracks and consider the best solution.

Critical reflection can firstly require recollection of a past event or experience. The second stage of reflection is the careful and objective observation of what has been recollected. Thirdly, critical reflection requires consideration of potential and alternative responses to the past event or experience until an appropriate response is found. On arrival at this possible solution, it is essential that there is then a halt. This pause allows us to return to the original data for any new observations or recollections, which can then be reconsidered in addition to any further alternative responses. The process can be repeated until there is a satisfactory resolution. Critical reflection can then inform subsequent action. This process involves an examination of beliefs, values, ideas, and behaviour. It necessarily involves challenging assumptions and personal views that are taken for granted. It requires making conscious that which is subconscious. This necessitates close scrutiny in order to gain a deeper understanding or to obliterate misunderstanding.

Brookfield (1987) also describes critical thinking in terms of phases, which can be applied to critical reflection. He says that there must be some type of catalyst to spur the thinker to become critical. This event must be examined and explored closely in order to gain an objective perspective of its origins. Alternative perspectives of the event can then be pursued and applied in future action. What is vital to this process is the exposure and challenging of assumptions that are intrinsic to the event recollected. These assumptions must be scrutinised carefully if there is to be authentic criticality. We may assume that our values and beliefs are personal, but they may be embedded in cultural assumptions and, therefore, part of an inherent and pervasive hegemony within society. Discovery of such assumptions can be disturbing as it may undermine our sense of self and individuality. This is not an easy process and may be resisted because '[i]f our thought structures are the ways in which we organize our perceptions to make sense of the world, it seems natural that we would have a strong vested interest in maintaining those structures' (Meyers, 1986, p. 96). Nevertheless, it is important that our structures are scrutinised because this task is 'central to thinking critically' and is 'at the heart of critical teaching' (Brookfield, 1987, pp. 89–90).

Similar to Dewey (1933), Boud et al. (1985) categorise critical reflective thinking in stages. The first stage is that of recollection or returning to a past event or experience. This is to gather data as objectively as possible through dispassionate observation. The second stage requires an acknowledgment and assessment of the emotions accompanying the event recalled. The third and final stage of critical reflection is the re-evaluating of the original event or experience. The ideal outcomes of this process are to achieve alternative perspectives on the event and a change in subsequent behaviour. This reiterates the idea of praxis (Freire, 1970) whereby reflection and action are interrelated. This idea is also found in literature on professional practice (Schön, 1987; 1991) where movement 'repeatedly back and forth between reflection on and in action' is recommended (Schön, 1987, p. 311). Reflection-on-action occurs when there is a 'trigger' event or when a routine action causes an unexpected result. Future action is then shaped by reflection on this event. Reflection and action are removed from each other and take place at different times. By contrast, reflection-in-action is where reflection and action take place together in space and time. A pertinent question is how the stages of critical reflection can be captured effectively for scrutiny. The use of 'critical incidents' is one example.

Critical incidents

A specific use of 'critical incidents' can be traced back to the Second World War, although the general methodology of collecting data of this kind originates from the nineteenth century. In 1941, there was an urgent need to undergo an appropriate selection of pilots and thus the critical incident technique arose through the American Aviation Psychology Program. Its use was not confined to pilots as they were later utilised for gathering information on different groups of workers, for example, dentists and sales assistants (Flanagan, 1954).

Basically, critical incidents concern 'procedures for collecting observed incidents having special significance and meeting systematically defined criteria' (Flanagan, 1954, p. 327). In this sense, it is primarily about the collection, rather than the analysis of data, and it certainly does not 'automatically provide solutions to problems' (p. 355). It is a technique or tool that can be used to aid critical reflection, from which a change in understanding, attitudes, beliefs, and behaviour may result. For the purposes of critical reflection, especially within service-learning or any other experiential learning or reflexive practice, critical incidents may be found easily once students understand what they are. A common misconception is that they must involve urgent life or death situations, whereas most critical incidents merely denote a turning point.

In service-learning, such incidents occur mostly while students are engaged in service to the community and where they may be unfamiliar with service users, staff, or routines of a service agency. Such incidents may be insignificant to, and possibly undetected by, other people, but they are critical to us because they represent a hiatus in our thinking or behaviour. A critical incident can be identified particularly easily if, for example, it is signified by the arising of discomfort, embarrassment, confusion, or puzzlement.

Critical incidents may begin with a dilemma, or what Dewey (1933) referred to metaphorically as a forked road where we are suddenly faced with an alternative route or course of action. In service-learning, this frequently occurs when students first engage with service in the community. As an example, there may be an occasion when a student is unclear as to how to behave among staff in a service agency, or what to say in response to a service-user. These situations provide opportunities for learning, especially if students recognise and acknowledge them as such. The critical incidents may arise from a minor event and may not be discernible to other people or indeed to the student herself. Initially, the nature of critical incidents is unearthed commonly through dialogue, when students discuss together their own and each other's experiences on placement. Such discovery can be cathartic and lead some students to prolific critical incident writing (Deeley, 2007).

The reporting of a critical incident therefore begins with recognising dissonance or a 'disorienting dilemma' (Mezirow, 1990, p. 14). At this stage, it is important merely to observe and describe the situation as objectively as possible. This, according to Brockbank and McGill (2007, pp. 126–7) is 'narrative reflection'. The critical incident technique may then require the student to consider their response to the event or to engage in 'percipient reflection' (pp. 126–7). What follows is some analysis of the data collection so far, in terms of relating the event to previous experience or learning. The next stage is to reflect on the potential responses that might have been made to the event and, with hindsight, to decide which would be the most appropriate. It is useful to consider the nature of the event and the possible reasons for its occurrence.

Finally, it is relevant to consider what implications there might be for the future, or how the critical reflection on the event can inform future events, responses, or behaviour. Clearly then, critical incidents are highly personal and are based largely on our own value judgements. As Tripp (1993, p. 12) affirms, '[W]e construct our world through reflection, but how and on what we reflect is largely determined by our existing world view'. Not only are critical incidents revealing: they also demonstrate the process of learning. Critical incidents allow 'insights into learners' assumptive worlds in expressions that are indisputably the learners' own' (Brookfield, 1990, p. 180). This is essential to understanding how and why the use of critical incidents can instigate change in learners. Through the process of critical reflection using the critical incident technique, the learners' hidden assumptions can be discovered. This may give rise to feelings of discomfort, which may, in turn, lead to acceptance and change in the individual, potentially to the degree of transformation. Equally, however, it could result in denial and rejection of any insight that may have occurred.

It is important within service-learning and useful in reflective practice that critical incidents are shared and open to discussion with others. A trusting and supportive learning environment is essential for this to occur effectively. It is through others shedding a different light on an event that insights can be gained.

A supportive learning environment

Critical reflection is both a solitary and a group activity. To begin, quiet time is needed rather than 'the dominant mode is primarily of noise and haste, rather than of space and silence' (Dawson, 2003, p. 33). A similar view is echoed by Alerby and Elídóttir (2003, p. 49), who assert that 'silence is often neglected as an important part of reflection in teaching and learning'. As such, it is important to develop the capacity for contemplation, or what Hart (2008, p. 237) refers to as 'interiority' which is 'almost entirely absent from contemporary education'.

The paths through interiority are solitary ones, but these can later be shared with others through dialogue to make sense and meaning of one's personal 'journeys to the interior'. It is part of the service-learning teacher's role to guide and assist this type of shared discussion within class. It is necessary for the class to be small in order for students to have the time and opportunity to participate fully, and also for trust to develop between them and between the students and the teacher. A large group can be intimidating for learners to speak out, especially if speaking out means revealing personal experiences and self-reflection. Mutual trust is an essential ingredient to critical reflection as a group activity. Another important factor is reciprocity. Supportive sharing in this way is useful for effective learning because '[u]nless we can accept that others have views very different from ours, and that a multiplicity of interpretations of practically every idea or action is possible, we will be unable to contemplate alternatives in our own thoughts and actions' (Brookfield, 1987, p. 241).

Group members, including the teacher, can validate each other's reflections on their experience as well as offering objective viewpoints. The success of the reflective tutorial group lies in the sum of its parts. Each member is significant in offering his or her contribution to the group's reflections. The prevalent attitudes within the group may also affect its success. It is important, for example, that each student is an active participant who gives other members of the group their active and full attention. Open mindedness and a willingness to accept alternative views and suggestions made by others are essential. An agreed class contract made at the beginning of a course is a useful device to ensure that learners agree how the class will function (Fook and Gardner, 2007). Further factors that contribute to the success of these groups are genuine interest and enthusiasm by each of the participants (Dewey, 1933). A high level of trust between the group members may be gained because of each one's need for confidentiality in revealing their personal reflections. It is vital that learners are encouraged and supported in their efforts to understand the meaning of others' experiences and vital to this is attentive listening. Open communication is essential to avoid ambiguity or misunderstanding. Support and validation of others' reflections are also necessary factors in the success of these groups in which the teacher plays a key role as facilitator. A major task of the teacher is to 'elicit the assumptions underlying (students') thoughts and actions' (Brookfield, 1987, p. 39) through a process of communal 'reflective analysis' (p. 93).

Potential outcomes of critical reflection

There are many factors involved when examining the potential outcomes of critical reflection. An outcome may depend on the purpose of critical reflection or there may be an unplanned and unexpected outcome. Fook and Gardner (2007, p. 143) outline possible outcomes of critical reflection from a work practice oriented perspective. These outcomes encompass cognitive, affective, and conative factors. Their study indicates that critical reflection can be utilised in various ways and is clearly not limited to an educational setting. Critical reflection is a skill transferable to the workplace. There are several potential outcomes that may occur as a result of critical reflection, but none is guaranteed. It is possible, however, that students may experience significant change.

Change

It is claimed that reflection is 'an active process of exploration and discovery which often leads to very unexpected outcomes' (Boud et al., 1985, p. 7). It could be expected that reflective activity potentially leads to change. There are no guarantees that change will occur, or the extent to which change might occur. It is pertinent to note also that 'not all change is transformative and not all critical reflection leads to transformative learning' (Grabove, 1997, p. 89). Much is dependent on individual students and their situations, thus the potential outcome of critical reflection is person, time, and place specific.

The outcome of critical reflection may be perceived suddenly as a catharsis. Alternatively, the outcome may be perceived gradually as a slow awakening. Indeed, potentially, the outcome may be a mixture of moments of change, some of which occur suddenly, while others evolve slowly. Quite often change may occur to an individual's perspective, the consequences of which may be positive or negative. This reiterates the ideas of Mezirow, as referred to in Chapters 3 and 4. He claims that what we think and understand is influenced and shaped by our own personal constructs of the world which consist of our habits and expectations. These can be acquired through socialisation and enculturalisation, learned intentionally or assimilated subconsciously. Our sense of self and self-esteem is inherent with our view of the world. If this view is disrupted through the process of critical reflection, it may have negative effects on our sense of well-being. As referred to earlier, there are ethical implications arising from the use of critical reflection within an academic setting. It is imperative that service-learning teachers, for example, are aware of the potential negative effects of critical reflection because of a duty of care and responsibility towards students. Negative effects can become a positive force, as Cranton (2006, p. 33) reminds us that '[r]eflection is a key concept in transformative learning theory'. It must be acknowledged, however, that this type of learning may not arise directly from critical reflection, but through the discomfort that accompanies it. As Mezirow (1991, p. 364) points out, students whose 'equilibrium has been upset by the advent of a dilemma...are in a state of readiness to learn anything that will ease their distress'.

Discomfort

Critical reflection can be a discomforting experience, or result in later discomfort. If our understanding and ways of interpreting ourselves, our experience, and the world are disrupted, this can cause uncertainty, fear, and loss of confidence. Our world can be shaken by critical reflection because it can involve facing one's 'own demons' (Deeley, 2007, p. 37). Certainly, our whole self-concept can be challenged by critical reflection as 'challenges and negations of our conventional criteria of self-assessment are always fraught with threat' (Mezirow, 1990, p. 12). This may contribute to students' resistance to, or rejection of, service-learning, as referred to earlier.

Discomfort can arise when our personal values are challenged: '[s]ometimes these painful and threatening learnings have to do with contradictions within oneself...Any learning which arises from this dilemma is painful and threatening since the two beliefs cannot openly co-exist, and any learning which emerges from the contradiction involves a definite change in the structure of self' (Rogers, 1969, p. 159). Nevertheless, discomfort may ultimately transmute into a positive experience. New insight and understanding can arise from the remaining ashes of negative experiences, as Rogers claims that 'all significant learning is to some degree painful and involves turbulence' (p. 339). To illustrate this, service-learning students have described the effects of their critical reflection as 'daunting...frightening' because 'it turns your world upside down' (Deeley, 2007, p. 32).

Another problem with critical reflection is that it may be difficult to stop this activity. Bulpitt and Martin (2005, p. 211) warn of this, saying that it is 'something that cannot always be turned on and off at will'. This was demonstrated by a student reporting some of the negative aspects of her experiences of critical reflection in service-learning, explaining that 'you can't shut off'. She said, 'I just need my mind to stop...it scares you, it kind of throws you off balance' (Deeley, 2007, p. 33). This demonstrates the importance of student support and the necessity of teaching students how to stop and detach from their critical reflections.

Construction of meaning

According to Boud et al. (1985) deep learning may be a consequence of a reflective approach in education. It is not surprising then that a major potential outcome of critical reflection is that of making meaning. It can include making sense of past experience, creating a new understanding of the present, and informing future action. In service-learning, critical reflection is the bridge that connects academic coursework with students' service in the community. It gives students the opportunity to stand on the metaphorical bridge between theory and practice, between the abstract and the concrete, between the general and the specific, and to encompass the entire vista within one frame. Critical reflection is the tool for students to make sense of their service-learning in their participation in service to the community as active citizens and co-operatively in the learning community of their student peers within reflective tutorials.

Through constructing meaning and gaining deeper insight, critical reflection may contribute to increased intellectual development. When engaged in critical discourse concerning their reflections, students may listen to, and learn from, each other. This may contribute to their awareness that varying perspectives may have equal validity and induce in students 'a willingness to critique one's own reasoning' (King and Kitchener, 1994, p. 71), which is of the highest level of reflective judgement. By recognising that there is frequently more than one answer or solution to any given question or problem, McEwen (1996, p. 62) claims that 'epistemic distortions' can thus be reduced or eliminated. To demonstrate an example of intellectual development resulting from engaging in critical reflection, a student claimed that critical reflection 'helped me to think more clearly about what I think and why' (Deeley, 2007). The process of development is encapsulated by another student who said, '[Y]ou're always assuming you're always right, your opinions are your own, in your own person you are right because that's what you think...(critical reflection in service-learning) got me thinking about it and it's still going through my head'.

It could be argued that critical reflection, especially if it concerns self-reflection, may nurture increased personal development, in addition to increased intellectual development. By learning to examine different alternatives and perspectives, an accelerated growth of maturity may ensue. As Brookfield (1987, p. x) astutely points out, 'Reflecting on the assumptions underlying our and others' ideas and actions, and contemplating alternative ways of thinking and living – is one of the important ways in which we become adults'.

Raised awareness

Making meaning may lead to new perspectives being gained which may result in increased awareness. For example, numerous service-learning students have commented that critical reflection had raised their awareness (Deeley, 2007). This increased awareness is an important factor in the process of raising consciousness and deepening understanding. With critical understanding, it is possible to recognise assumptions, taken for granted values and beliefs, cultural influences, and pervasive societal hegemony. Only when these issues are recognised can they be challenged. Critical reflection is a tool that can be used for this purpose. As one service-learning student reported, 'It makes me so aware of everything...about making judgements, and assumptions about oppression and discrimination, and institutionalised and internalised oppression' (Deeley, 2007).

The recognition and acknowledgment of oppression as a result of raised awareness is liberating and produces integrated knowledge and understanding (Belenky et al., 1997). For women, in particular, this is important because it is congruent with a feminist perspective. Freire (1970) is also concerned with raising consciousness with a view to emancipation, believing that through educational means it is possible to raise awareness to the level of critical consciousness. Thus, through critical reflection, conscientisation may be achieved as discussed in the previous chapter. This may also lead to transformative learning, as discussed earlier.

Praxis

Both Dewey (1938) and Freire (1970) advocate praxis, which can be interpreted as the combination of critical thinking and critical action. Praxis can also mirror the experiential learning cycle where critical thinking can lead to critical action. Consequently, this is closely associated with community or political action for social justice. Critical reflection can raise awareness of societal injustice and the need for more engaged and active citizenship. Here, there is a role for service-learning as a critical pedagogy, which was explored in Chapter 4. This also resonates with the claim by Brookfield (1987, p. 3) that '[c]ivically, a critically informed populace is seen as more likely to participate in forms of democratic political activity'.

Interestingly, Barnett (1997) contends that nurturing critical thinkers as an aim of higher education is actually insufficient and that students' critical thinking should be transmuted into action. Critical thinkers may then become critical actors, to instigate change: either in self, society, or both. Barnett advocates that this process should evolve as the holistic growth of critical beings. He says that '[t]he university precisely has a responsibility, qua university, to develop the capacity within its students to take up critical stances in the world and not just towards the world' (p. 112). Critical reflection is part of this complex process.

Critical reflection and service-learning

Throughout this chapter, reference has been made to the associations between service-learning and critical reflection. Indeed, critical reflection is essential to this type of experiential learning. Service-learning, in combining academic coursework with service to the community, connects theory with practice and the abstract with the concrete. It involves personal experience and how this contributes to, and shapes, students' learning. Service-learning thus differs from traditional pedagogy in that it is active learning through experience. As Jacques (2000, p. 54) shrewdly emphasises, 'Learning is not a spectator sport'. This has implications for teachers because they no longer become the '(mere) purveyors of data' (Harvey and Knight, 1996, p. 155). The potential effects of critical reflection in service-learning, and on teachers and their role, are explored here.

The role of critical reflection

As stated earlier, critical reflection is an activity that is intrinsic to service-learning. Students must construct meaning from their own experiences of giving service to the community and connecting it to the academic coursework. To do this requires critical reflection. As Boud (2001, p. 10) explains, 'Reflection involves taking the unprocessed raw material of experience and engaging with it as a way to make sense of what has occurred'. Critical reflection, therefore, is the ligament that connects the two bones which are academic study and service to the community. An example of how this might function could be a student's critical reflection on her service experience in a women's rape crisis centre and how it relates to the academic study of women's oppression and theories of domestic violence. Another example might be a student's critical reflection of her service experience in a hospice and the academic study of policies and ethical issues relating to palliative care, dying, and euthanasia. It is imperative to identify and acknowledge the theoretical dimension of service-learning because, as Hart (1990, p. 67) explains, '[t]heoretical knowledge must at some point become an explicit concern because it supplies the general tools that can make transparent the relations that obtain among isolated and fragmented incidents of personal experience'.

Critical reflection allows for the personal to enter into the formal academic environment. It necessitates the individuality of each student to interpret or challenge generally accepted knowledge, assumptions, and their experiences in order to construct meaning. Critical reflection is also the launching pad for praxis and the transference of thought into action. For service-learning students this can include personal change, becoming more active citizens in their communities, as well as perhaps instigating societal and political change. The potential consequences are wide, varying, and perhaps limitless. Critical reflection is also transferable skill that students can use in their future employment, which is discussed in Chapter 7.

The role of the teacher

Reciprocity is a major theme evident in service-learning (Deeley, 2004). Communities may benefit from students' service to the community by volunteering in a welfare agency. In return, students also benefit by their learning from this experience. It is 'an exchange: it involves giving and receiving. This reciprocity is linked to interdependence' (p. 216). Reciprocity has been identified as a prevalent characteristic of the tripartite relationships between student, agency, and university; and between student, staff, and service-users (Deeley, 2004). It can be further claimed, however, that reciprocity also exists between student and teacher. Indeed, as far as facilitating and nurturing critical reflection, authenticity has primacy. In this sense, reciprocity is essential in terms of communication, trust, and taking risks. There is an element of potential vulnerability when students discuss their reflective thoughts because they reveal personal views. Teachers are responsible for creating an atmosphere of trust and support among students (Bringle and Hatcher, 1999; Brockbank and McGill, 2007; Elliott-Kemp and Rogers, 1982). The teacher's willingness to set an example of reflective thinking by some self-disclosure is helpful in building trust in the classroom, in addition to encouraging a more democratic classroom to evolve. Reiterating the theme of reciprocity, this situation 'requires a great deal of effort, courage, and authenticity on the part of both the educator and the learner, because there is considerable risk and the effort may or may not result in reward' (Grabove, 1997, p. 90).

There is a dearth of research on the effects on teachers who facilitate and engage in critical reflection with students in the classroom, as teachers must challenge their own assumptions in the same way as students. In service-learning, if teachers are to become more democratic they must face the thorny issue of whether or not it is appropriate that they participate in giving service to the community alongside their students and engage in critical reflection on their experiences also. If teachers become as students in this sense, then they, too, must face the possibility that they might experience discomfort in the critical reflective process. It is a risky endeavour. As referred to earlier, the teacher may be required to climb down from the lofty pedestal of knowledge and face her students on level ground. Student empowerment implies that the teacher relinquishes some of her power. This is a pertinent factor in transformative education as Cranton (1994, p. 91) claims that '[l]earner empowerment is...the ultimate goal of transformative learning and of adult education'.

Reflecting critically on their role in the classroom is good practice for service-learning teachers. As Shor (1987, p. 101) admits, the 'liberatory learning process is very demanding on the teacher'. Preparation for classes is essential, but the teacher must also be prepared to abandon lesson plans according to how the class proceeds. The teacher must be a keen and sensitive listener in order to hear what is not said, as well as what is said, when students share their critical reflections. This allows the teacher to detect any underlying emotions emanating from her students. Inevitably, the teacher becomes embroiled in a 'matrix of roles and functions' (p. 102) to the point where she becomes 'a participant learner' (Rogers, 1969, p. 165) in a milieu of mutuality and reciprocity. A democratic classroom may be impossible to achieve because the teacher inherently retains power through her professional role and the academic assessment processes which award credit for students' coursework. Nevertheless, a more democratic sharing of power can be established. This is referred to further in Chapters 6 and 7.

Conclusion

This chapter has examined critical reflection because of its essential role in service-learning. Critical reflection is a critical thinking skill that belongs to the heart of higher education and is transferable to the workplace. The meaning of critical reflection has been examined through various lenses, beginning with an exploration of thinking itself, drawing on the work of Dewey and referring to different models of critical reflection. Leading on from the premise in the previous chapter that service-learning can be perceived as a critical pedagogy, the connections between critical reflection, the process of conscientisation, and praxis have been examined. Inevitably, it is through the process of critical reflection that change may occur, which may ultimately lead to transformative learning. The effects of critical reflection may potentially extend from personal change in beliefs, attitudes, and behaviour to wider societal change. The processes and stages of critical reflection have also been explored with potential methods of its facilitation, including the necessity of a supportive learning environment and the use of critical incidents, which are also discussed in Chapters 6 and 7.

The potential outcomes of critical reflection which may give rise to change have also been examined. A prevalent negative factor of critical reflection is discomfort, whereas a more positive one is students' raised awareness. The symbiosis of critical reflection with service-learning was also made explicit and the inherently influential key role of the teacher was discussed.

This chapter on critical reflection paves the way for further discussion on important issues within service-learning. These issues concern academic reflective writing and appropriate, constructively aligned assessment that may be utilised to capture students' critical reflections effectively. These are the topics of the following chapters.

6
Academic Writing in Service-Learning

Introduction

The previous chapter was concerned with critical reflection: defining its meaning and role within service-learning; facilitating its use; and examining its potential consequences. This chapter delves deeper into this vital aspect of service-learning by focusing on how critical reflection can be ensnared from the ephemeral and abstract world of unseen thought to the material world through the medium of academic writing. This chapter demonstrates how critical incidents and journal writing can be used in critical thinking and reflective processes. Although the focus in this chapter is on writing in service-learning, it is also applicable to other types of experiential learning and reflective practice.

Service-learning is a non-traditional pedagogy, underpinned by experiential learning theory. As such, it involves students as active learners, constructing meaning in order to make sense of the experiences of their service to the community and to connect these experiences to the academic coursework. The community experience is unforeseen, unlike a controlled and structured academic syllabus. Each individual student takes to her placement a host of prior learning, assumptions, and expectations which will affect her community service. It follows that two students placed at the same agency are likely to have different experiences, or at least produce different interpretations of their experience. Such is the individual and unpredictable nature of service-learning. It is important, therefore, for the teacher to create a scaffold for students' learning by offering supportive guidance, modelling, and formative feedback. Tutorial discussions and the processes of reflective writing are the contexts within which learning can be enhanced. As service-learning is unconventional in its approach, it is appropriate that its assessment methods are aligned to this type of learning. Indeed, service-learning can provide teachers with the opportunities to step outside the boundaries of traditional learning and teaching methods and assessment (Deeley, 2013).

The experiential learning nature of service-learning consists of service to the community and the learning that derives from that service coupled with academic theory. Ideally then, service (practice) is informed by learning (theory) and learning (theory) is informed by service (practice). The major tool for executing the connections between academic coursework and the inevitably ill-structured practical experience of a placement in the community is critical reflection. This leads to the main purpose of this chapter, which is to explore academic writing in service-learning that allows students to demonstrate their learning through service-learning and the critical and reflective processes they have developed. Students, therefore, must be able to demonstrate the final outcome of their learning, but vitally they must also reveal the path by which they arrived and where it might further lead. Critical reflection is a metacognitive process in which students discover how they learn.

This chapter focuses on academic writing in service-learning because it differs from what is usually expected in conventional methods of learning and teaching in higher education. This factor will be examined with reference to the literature concerning the use of the narrative and the construction of personal storytelling. It is important for students to overcome intellectual and emotional barriers to writing in a personal style. Initially, students may resist this if they are imbued with the idea that only writing in an impersonal style is acceptable in higher education. If students do not overcome their resistance, a general difficulty with, and rejection of, service-learning may transpire. Nevertheless, students invariably grasp that to succeed in this type of academic course they must adopt a different style of writing in order to demonstrate their learning. For some, this path can be illuminated by the excitement which can be generated by the prospect of developing creativity and self-expression. Alternatively, the path may be darkened by clouds of uncertainty and anxiety as students may fear potential failure to meet academic expectations.

In order to facilitate an informed approach by students to their academic writing in service-learning, this chapter seeks to explore various aspects and implications of using the narrative and engaging in reflective writing. Furthermore, it attempts to demonstrate how critical reflection of service and learning may be expressed effectively through academically assessed assignments. In this chapter, the implications of academic writing in service-learning are explored in terms of student learning and the assessment of their learning. As personal experience is an integral part of this experiential learning process, ethical issues concerning the type and level of personal disclosure that may arise are discussed.

Reflective writing is an integral part of service-learning and serves two purposes. Firstly, it is used as a means of facilitating critical reflection and learning. Secondly, it is used for assessment as a requirement for academic credit. Students are not assessed for their voluntary work in the community per se. Instead, they are assessed for the written assignment resulting from their critical reflection on their service in the community and the connections this has with conceptual ideas within the academic coursework. To enable students to practise critical reflection of their experiences and to write about the process of critical reflection, it is useful to introduce short exercises in the form of critical incidents as referred to in Chapter 5. These can be used as formative assessment, or assessment for learning, which is good practice (Jessop et al., 2012; Nicol and McFarlane-Dick, 2006). They can also be used as summative assessment, which is often referred to as assessment of learning. In addition to writing about critical incidents, students are usually required to write a reflective journal as part of their service-learning assessed coursework.

This chapter will, therefore, examine the use of the narrative and reflective writing. Included here are authentic examples of students' written work taken from my service-learning classes in a Scottish university. Abbs (1974, p. 23) asserts that 'we cannot ask others to risk themselves in the name of education, unless we have done so or are willing to ourselves'. I have adopted this stance as part of my philosophy of learning and teaching and I ask students to do only what I have done, or am prepared to do, myself. Service-learning is no exception. Consequently, I have participated in voluntary work as part of service-learning both at home and abroad, with the former being undertaken concurrently with my students during a service-learning course that I was teaching at the time, and the latter being undertaken in Thailand after participating in an international service-learning conference. My service experiences were invaluable as they provided insight and a deeper understanding of service-learning, which has given me long lasting resonance with students' experiences. These experiences also helped me to model authentic examples of academic writing in service-learning to my students, which are referred to here. A further consequence of my service experiences was to adopt a more democratic approach in my teaching. Guiding students rather than directing them is pivotal to the success of service-learning pedagogy.

The chapter moves on to examine the process of writing critical incidents. It can be argued that this is an example of a structured approach to critical reflection and serves to enhance students' skills in journal writing. An example of a critical incident from my international service experience is included. This model is used to demonstrate and explain how a critical incident may be written. Following this, and with written informed consent, an example of a service-learning student's own critical incident is given. Critical incident writing can be used both as formative and as summative forms of assessment.

Participating in service to the community allowed me to provide students with examples of reflective writing taken from my own journals. As part of my pedagogical research on service-learning, which has ethical approval from the University of Glasgow, examples of students' own work, with their informed consent, is included in this chapter. These excerpts demonstrate students' critical reflections and the connections they made between their service and the academic coursework. All the students' work and any references to the staff and service-users within the community agencies are anonymous.

Reflective journal writing is a learning process which also results in an end product that can be used for assessment of their learning. In my service-learning teaching, students keep a private 'working' journal or diary to record their experiences and reflections. Subsequently, students utilise this data to write a 'formal' academic journal which is summatively assessed. A journal entry from my service abroad is given as an example to students and is included here. This is then followed by a series of different journal entries made by eight service-learning students between 2006 and 2013. The purpose of this is to exemplify different stages within a reflective journal (Chisholm, 2000). These stages are designed to give structure to students' critical reflections on their, invariably ill-structured, experiences of service to the community. By offering various excerpts from students' journal writing exemplifies the rich diversity of experience in service-learning.

Writing for learning and assessment

Academic writing in service-learning offers students an opportunity to be creative and to write in a style different from more conventional assignments commonly found in higher education, such as essays and reports. The use of the personal narrative is essential in service-learning because intrinsic to students' learning is their experience. Maintaining an academic writing style remains an imperative because the written assignments must conform to accepted academic standards. Thus, writing in service-learning must achieve two objectives. The first of these objectives is to demonstrate evidence of critical reflection on placement experience and the second is to demonstrate critical thinking which connects the conceptual and theoretical ideas in the academic coursework with the students' experiences. Students' reactions to what is expected from them in their service-learning assignments may range from apprehension to great excitement as is shown in the next chapter, but what is certain is that boredom in writing is rarely reported. Service-learning moves away from passive learning and 'mass-produce(d) knowledge' that can give rise to a 'deep inertia…a mindless torpor – or what might better be described as a pathology of boredom' (Abbs, 1974, p. 2).

It could be argued that traditional assessment methods such as essays and examinations are inappropriate for assessing the active learning that is found in service-learning. Finding effective and aligned assessment for service-learning might seem problematic. Compounding this issue are other factors such as ensuring validity and reliability in the assessment of students' critical and reflective thinking skills. In addition, ethical issues may rise from students writing from personal experience. A balance must be struck to safeguard, on the one hand, appropriate disclosure and, on the other hand, authenticity. What this infers is that students may take a strategic approach in their writing in order to achieve a high grade and adopt an approach which could result in a disingenuous narrative.

Each service-learning student has a unique learning experience, some of which is off campus and can be unpredictable. Their service in the community may be ill-structured and somehow students must make sense of this. They must transmute their experiences into learning by means of critical reflection on their placement experiences and the coursework. Discussion in class with the teacher and their student peers can enable learning by giving it structure and through a process of sharing, enhance students' understanding. This echoes Allard et al. (2007, p. 307) who 'found that when participants made their thinking and reflection visible to others, they opened the door for learning'. From another perspective, this process is also similar to narrative therapy developed by White and Epston (1990, in 'The Guardian', 2008) in which an individual's experiences are perceived as a series of stories and where problems are externalised.

Nevertheless, the vital and fundamental element in this process is critical thinking, of which critical reflection is an integral part. With critical thinking, ideas and assumptions that may be taken for granted can be challenged. This can be achieved through dialogue within a service-learning tutorial. Challenges to the hegemony, therefore, can involve social as well as individual processes. From a constructivist perspective, new meanings may emerge both collectively and individually. In a group setting, students can be encouraged to examine critically their assumptions to enable them to critically reflect and reconstruct their understanding. Support in this process is referred to as 'scaffolding' (Samuels and Betts, 2007, p. 271).

Assignments that 'relate to real problems and issues and draw upon students' own experiences' (Meyers, 1986, p. 73) are effective methods of assessing students' critical thinking skills. Relating practical real life examples to theoretical conceptualisations, as evident in service-learning, is a powerful approach to developing criticality. It is a process that is best tackled in incremental stages because critical thinking and critical reflection are skills that need to be learned, practised, and developed over time (Bruster and Peterson, 2013; Newton, 2004). Academic writing in service-learning demands a reflective approach which 'is a good way to foster critical thinking' (Bruster and Peterson, 2013, p. 180).

Ethical issues

Academic writing in service learning involves more than a demonstration of depersonalised critical thought and argument because there is an additional affective dimension to students' learning. This can be seen through students' placement experiences during their service to the community. There are, however, ethical issues of concern that arise from this. Firstly, it could be argued that personal development ought not to be assessed per se and, indeed, that it is difficult to assess reliably. A counterargument to this stance, however, is that personal development encompasses many facets, for example, it might include students' development of graduate attributes and employability skills, which can be assessed effectively. This aspect is investigated in depth in the next chapter.

A second ethical issue that may arise from the assessment of academic writing in service-learning, in particular journal writing, is that of students' privacy in terms of self-disclosure. Students may be perceived as being in a vulnerable position, especially as there are likely to be additional assessors who are unknown to the students, such as second markers and external examiners, so that '[t]he issue of audience with respect to journal writing is perhaps the most serious ethical question confronting adult education today' (English, 2001, p. 30). To counteract this ethical dilemma, students do have choices about, and control over, what they include in their assignments. In light of this, students' personal diaries and fieldwork journals ought not to be available for examiners' scrutiny. Linked to the issue of self-disclosure is another ethical matter of disclosure concerning a third party. In students' written assignments, references to welfare agencies in the community and to any staff and service-users within the agencies must be anonymised. Likewise, reflective tutorials must have an agreement of confidentiality within the group.

Although there may be risks associated with academic writing in service-learning because it involves personal as well as intellectual processes, the process of reflective writing is part of learning and is inextricably intertwined with constructive and supportive dialogue in class. Assignments must be tailored specifically to the aims and intended learning outcomes of the course, so the use of less conventional methods of assessment are appropriate. These can be used formatively to help students learn, and summatively, which may also help students learn, but essentially contributes to their final course grades. Academic writing in service-learning may include critical incidents, as referred to in the last chapter, and reflective journals. These two types of assignment are examined here.

Writing critical incidents

As referred to in the previous chapter, the use of critical incidents is not new. It stems from an event that causes us to stop in our tracks, for example, in Dewey's (1933) metaphor of reaching a 'forked road' and being unsure of which direction to take. It re-appears in Mezirow's (1991, p. 193) idea of a 'disorienting dilemma'. An event that is deemed critical refers to a point where a change occurs. The incident is whatever triggers that particular point. They do not necessarily represent 'a traumatic crisis', but rather 'any significant event that leaves the participant to feel puzzled or unclear about the incident and the outcome' (Hickson, 2011, p. 833). Critical incidents can appear as insignificant moments as 'they are mostly straightforward accounts of very commonplace events' (Tripp, 1993, pp. 24–5). Consequently they can be overlooked and initially difficult for students to discover. Critical incidents must be sought out (Tripp, 1993) and reflective tutorials provide ideal settings for this activity where students can help each other to identify them. Students have expressed their epochal understanding of critical incidents as the 'light bulb moment' (Deeley, 2007). In a reflective tutorial, for example, one of my students had initial difficulty in grasping the meaning of a critical incident and was thus unable to identify any in his placement. He narrated his reflections to the class until one student candidly pointed out a critical incident that was evident in his story. Consequently, the immediate and sudden dawning of his understanding was obvious by his expression and another student's exclamation of 'the penny's dropped!' resounded throughout the class, quickly followed by peals of laughter and a sense of relief that was almost tangible.

It is important to understand that the nature of a critical incident and how we respond to it depends on our interpretations, perceptions, and beliefs. We need to be objective about our subjective experiences in order to make authentic and critical evaluations in the context of our critical incidents. This enables us to raise our awareness of what has been, what could have been, and what might be in the future. It further allows an opportunity for us to challenge our assumptions and discover how easy it is for us to succumb to societal hegemony, pressures and expectations.

As referred to in the previous section, critical thinking and critical reflection are skills that must be learned and practised. Writing critical incidents is a tool for learning and a skill that can be developed usefully as a basis for further reflection in journal writing. A critical incident report, for example, can be presented as a series of questions that help students to structure their reflections. In this way, critical incidents may thus represent 'structured uncertainty' (Hickson, 2011, p. 836) as the questions enable students' deconstruction of events. Subsequently, this allows students' close analysis which may reveal their previously hidden assumptions. When these have been identified, their assumptions can then be challenged. The questions in a critical incident report can then probe students for evaluation of their action in the event and can encourage them to consider their future potential action, informed by this learning incident. This process mirrors a basic experiential learning cycle that begins with an experience, moves to reflection on that experience, followed by an evaluation of how this experience will inform future action and completes the cycle by moving towards the next experience. The aim of a critical incident is to raise students' awareness by providing a structured process to analyse events from which they can learn. This learning from experience is transferable to graduate employment and lifelong learning, for example, in professional practice and development (Schön, 1987; 1991).

Using critical incidents in teaching can be very useful (Brookfield, 2012a), but caution should be exercised if they are used as part of coursework assessment. As referred to earlier, a matter of particular concern is an ethical risk of students disclosing inappropriate personal issues. Another factor concerns the possible effects of using critical incidents in teaching because they may cause disequilibrium to a student's perspectives or belief system. This could create a negative stimulus for students which causes discomfort because critical reflection is 'not a dispassionate learning process... (it can be) a threatening encounter that challenges one's very "selfhood"' (Meyers, 1986, p. 96). Empirical evidence from service-learning research has demonstrated that students may indeed experience discomfort, for example, a student claimed that it was scary, as referred to in Chapter 5.

Alternatively, it could be argued that disequilibrium is a positive force from which effective and deep learning may occur. Some might argue further that such a force could result in transformation, as Cranton (1994, pp. 185–6) believes that '[c]ritical incidents can provide a powerful vehicle for stimulating transformative learning precisely because they are so closely connected to personal experience'. The aim of using critical incidents in service-learning, however, is to enhance learning rather than to deliberately and actively attempt to facilitate students' transformation. This is a different ethical concern, which is discussed in Chapter 8.

Critical incidents are basically concerned with the collection of data rather than the solving of specific problems (Flanagan, 1954). Nevertheless, they provide an opportunity for students to critically analyse the event and others' and their own reactions or responses; and to consider how the event itself and their critical reflection on it might alter their future behaviour, thoughts, or action. Students' written responses can be assessed for quality and depth of critical analysis. Critical incidents, therefore, can be useful and are appropriate as both formative and summative assessment. In particular, critical incident writing serves a useful purpose as part of service-learning assessment in higher education. It provides an opportunity for students to reflect on events in their service placement, to make sense of their experiences, and to learn from them. The experiential aspect of service-learning can be largely unpredictable so giving students a structural framework on which to hang their puzzling encounters allows space for them to iron out unexpected anomalies. It presents students with the opportunity to challenge their own taken for granted assumptions, encourages them to be inquisitive about others' perceptions and behaviour, and how these factors might influence others' assumptions. Moreover, critical incident writing allows students to structure their critical reflection, develop heightened awareness and deeper understanding.

Writing about critical incidents requires a collection of data which has then to be observed, interpreted and explained. Firstly, there must be a recollection of an event that holds some significance. As mentioned earlier, the event may appear initially as being insignificant or go unnoticed by others and may occur within a period of mere seconds. Secondly there must be a descriptive narrative that gives context to the event, which 'sets the scene'. The event is a snapshot and for effective writing, there must be a clear focus with clarity and succinctness in students' writing. Secondly, students must relate the immediate consequences of the event, which includes a record of their own response to it. Thirdly, students must engage in analytical reflection whereby they identify potential alternative responses to the event in terms of their action, speech, behaviour, or attitude. Engaging in evaluative reflection, students must then choose what course of action, in the specific circumstances of his event, would have been the most appropriate and effective. Using critical reflection, students must subsequently summarise the possible root causes of the event and identify inlaid hidden assumptions framing it. Finally, using their metacognitive skills, students must demonstrate how they have learned from the event and postulate how it will inform their future action (Brockbank and McGill, 2007, pp. 126–7). This strategy resonates with Dewey's (1933) analysis of reflective thinking that includes the recollection and observation of a past experience, including its context, and an examination of possible courses of future action. It also mirrors experiential learning cycles (Beard and Wilson, 2002; Kolb, 1993).

As 'it is good practice to use both formative and summative assessment methods' (Deeley, 2014, p. 40) to enhance student learning, examples of critical incidents can be used throughout students' service-learning experiences for their structured practice in the critical reflection process. It is helpful for students to be familiar with the assessment methods so offering models or examples of critical incident reports is most beneficial. I use examples of critical incidents from my own voluntary work service-learning experience abroad in Thailand and at home in the United Kingdom as models to facilitate students' understanding of critical incidents. Interestingly, during an explanation and deconstruction of an example of a critical incident, I slowly became aware that my students did not realise that

I had written it. I had assumed that the critical incident was clearly about my experience and this mistaken assumption became a critical incident for me within the classroom. Some students had openly criticised how the author had reflected and acted in the incident and their comments were refreshingly and surprisingly honest. Their comments led me to reflect again on the incident. Later revealing that I was in fact the author of the critical incident caused a stir with the students as they recalled their outspoken comments with embarrassment. The students' mistaken assumption was a critical incident for them. Here is the example I used.

A critical incident abroad

The incident

My service placement took place immediately following a service-learning conference in Thailand. One day during my placement I visited a Buddhist temple accompanied by a monk. We arrived at the temple, having walked there together observing the acceptable physical distance between us according to the conventions of Thai Buddhism. I wanted to take a photograph of him so he kindly obliged and sat in a meditation position in front of a very large statue of the Buddha. I then asked him if he would take a photograph of me in the temple. He agreed, and so I offered him my camera. At this point, however, he took a step back and didn't take the camera from me. It was an awkward moment.

My response

At first I was puzzled and embarrassed as I didn't understand why he had stepped away from me. I then thought he might have misunderstood my request because of our language difference, although I wasn't convinced by this idea because he spoke English fluently. Nevertheless, I offered the camera to him again and this time he clearly refused to take it. The reason then dawned on me as I recalled that he was prohibited from taking anything directly from a woman. As a monk, he was not allowed to touch, or risk touching, a woman and, therefore, he would not take the camera from me. I realised that I would have to put the camera on the ground so that he could then 'safely' take it.

How I might have responded

Part of this convention requires monks to keep a physical distance from women and I had been aware of that as we had walked with a short distance between us. I should have remembered this in the temple when I asked him to take a photograph, and I ought to have put my camera on the ground immediately so that he could then pick it up.

What might have been the best response

The best response would have been to ask him to take a photograph and put the camera down immediately. This would have saved us both from unnecessary embarrassment.

The real problem

Part of the problem was due to our cultural and social differences and the imposed rules and regulations associated with an organised religion. It also involved different assumptions concerning social etiquette and the motivation underlying another's behaviour. Another part of the problem was my not being mindful of my actions. In admiration of the temple and a wish to take photographs, I had temporarily forgotten the conventions to which he adhered. Ironically, a similar event occurred at the end of my stay. As I was at the airport waiting for my flight departure, the monk arrived unexpectedly with an entourage of other monks and academic staff to wish me goodbye. He had brought a farewell gift which he offered to me directly, but then suddenly and clearly embarrassed, he quickly withdrew it as he remembered that this was forbidden. Smiling at his own error, he turned to his male colleague who was not a monk, and asked him to give it to me instead.

How my learning from this incident will affect my future action

This incident reveals a level of my ethnocentrism of which I became aware after I had assumed that I could give my camera directly to the monk. The awkwardness this generated and my subsequent reflections will lead me to acting in a more ethnorelative manner (Pusch, 2004).

An example of a student's critical incident (Student A)

The incident

It was my first day of service to frail elderly people in the community (hereafter referred to as 'service-users'), and I had just been introduced to them, staff carers, and volunteers. I was going around the room and trying to get to know a few of the service-users when one of the carers asked if I could help with moving the breakfast tables so that we could begin the morning activities. I approached the nearest table and as I began to lift it one of the service-users screamed out, 'No! What are you doing?' Her shout was so loud that the room was suddenly silent. She continued to shout out as I continued to stand, frozen, holding the table.

My response

My response was one of shock, as I had not expected anyone to react so strongly to a table being moved. From this point I seemed to completely freeze, I was still standing holding the table as the carer instructed me again to take it away, whilst the service-user kept screaming out 'No!' I was standing frozen, hoping that someone would intervene or come to my rescue. At this point I felt really uncomfortable and given that I had only been in the service agency for around an hour, I felt completely embarrassed.

How I might have responded

A more effective response may have been to put down the table, to approach the service-user who seemed distressed by this and listen to her concern/s. This would hopefully have reassured the service-user and from this point I could have moved the table and the activities could have begun. If this had failed I could also have asked one of the carers for help or guidance on what to do, the carers did not know my previous experience (or lack of it) so they may have assumed I was comfortable dealing with this incident.

What might have been the best response

I believe it is clear that the course of action that I took only made the situation worse for everyone. I should have been far more pro-active and listened to the service-user's concerns with my moving the table, and hopefully from this point I could have reassured her. I believe this would have been the best course of action as it would have calmed her, resulting in my being able to carry out the very basic task that I had been asked to complete.

The real problem

I believe there were several factors that contributed to the real problem in this incident. Firstly, I now realise through experience that the service-user in question has Alzheimer's, and this can lead such patients to experiencing days where they are confused over their whereabouts and the people around them. All that was required was to speak to her, attempt to reassure her, and not to back off and appear scared, which only exacerbated the situation. I also believe that I had a lack of confidence in my ability to deal with the situation. My lack of confidence to respond led to me panicking and offering no help to the service-user. It may also be true that fear played a part in this incident: I did not react because I was worried how the service-user, who was already shouting at me, would react.

How my learning from this incident will affect my future action

I hope that through reflection and experience my future action will be far more pro-active. I have learned, and actively try to build up a rapport with each service-user on a weekly basis, hoping to learn more about them and any needs that they might have. Hopefully this means I am more of use to the service-users and staff in this case. I also believe that my lack of confidence in this scenario played a huge role in my poor response to this situation. As the weeks pass I grow more confident in my role at the service agency. I hope that an increasing confidence coupled with a developing rapport with several of the service-users will result in me not worrying about intervening in any challenging situations in the future. Finally, I believe that having an understanding that many of the service-users are affected by Alzheimer's and that some days can be more challenging than others, will make me more aware of how a simple task may result in distress to a service-user, I must ensure that I react to this positively and that I am not afraid to approach the service-user.

Reflective journals

Through the process and structure of writing critical incidents, students gain valuable experience of writing reflectively. A fuller account of their service-learning is achieved, however, through reflective journal writing. The process of writing a journal serves to enable students' learning in addition to providing evidence of their learning which can be assessed for the purpose of gaining coursework credit.

For quality in learning and teaching, it is of value that the aims, intended learning outcomes or objectives, and assessment of a course are mutually suited. In service-learning, critical incidents and reflective journals are both 'constructively aligned' (Biggs and Tang, 2011, p. 97) to the nature of this pedagogy. Journal writing as an assessment method is appropriate for service-learning because a reflective journal is a product that represents a process of learning. Service-learning is experiential and holistic, which means that learning is individualised and personal, involving an affective dimension. Journal writing allows for the expression of individuality and retains the capacity for critical analysis expected in academic writing in higher education. Reflective writing in journals encourages the process of critical thinking, which reveals that writing a journal is part of the learning process. The journal is also a product that, when written according to academic standard conventions, can also be assessed. Serving the two purposes of a process and a product (Rainer, 1978), journals are of ideal use in service-learning. The remaining part of this chapter will examine the writing, learning, and assessment of reflective journals.

Writing a reflective journal

For academic credit, students' reflective journals must demonstrate critical analysis, knowledge and understanding. The journal should encapsulate and make sense of the combination of students' ill-structured service experience on placement, the structured tutorial discussions, and study of academic coursework of theoretical and abstract conceptualisations. This is a major task. As referred to earlier, the journal is a process of making meaning and it is a product of students' learning which can be assessed. It is important that criteria for the journal are clearly understood by students. Marking criteria for a service-learning journal and advice for students is referred to in a later section of this chapter.

Acknowledging and bearing in mind that certain criteria must be met for assessment purposes, writing a journal entails a process of 'cognitive housekeeping' explained as 're-organizing knowledge and emotional orientations in order to achieve further insights' (Moon, 2006, p. 37). The element of personal experience make the journal what Hettich (1976, p. 60) refers to as a 'topical autobiography' which is described as a 'short discontinuous personal document which represents the excerpting from an individual's life of a special class of events'. In other words, writing a journal is a way of narrating a story, which can also be a 'powerful learning tool' (McDrury and Alterio, 2003, p. 7). Telling one's own story of service-learning involves recalling past events and making sense of them for one's self and for others. This is a learning process that is directly relevant to students' own experience and is conducive to deep learning. Indeed, service-learning in this respect is advantageous because generally '[e]ducators have been rather slow to see the potential of autobiographical and other personal reports on learning' (Powell, 1985, p. 42).

Part of this type of learning involves shared dialogue during reflective tutorials and written analysis within journals. The feasibility of relating theory to experience demands some structure which can be achieved through the natural progress of a story. Through the mask of narration and the use of metaphor, students may feel less vulnerable to, or intimidated by, potential self-disclosure. Journal writing in the mode of a tale lends students an opportunity to step back from their experience and view it more objectively and critically. This may also help them make connections between theory and practice. McDrury and Alterio (2003, p. 175) claim that this genre is appropriate in higher education, saying that 'when we encourage students to articulate and process experience through storytelling we provide them with opportunities to clarify and question their assumptions ... storytelling can, and should, be viewed as a theory of learning'. Using a narrative has 'the potential to provoke reflection on practice' (Smith and Squire, 2007, p. 376). In addition, the 'narrative provides order, structure and direction ... and helps develop meanings in richer and more integrated ways' (Gill, 2014, p. 33). Journal writing can be an effective process for learning.

In narrating a tale, the writing style and language in a reflective journal differ from that normally used by students in other forms of academic writing in higher education. In addition, writing about personal experiences may be alien to students and consequently they may find it difficult (Rainer, 1978). The use of metaphors can alleviate such difficulties in students' academic journal writing. Metaphors in storytelling may help towards making meaning by offering complex ways of interpreting experience (Semino, 2014) and, according to Beard and Wilson (2006, p. 207), 'can provide another way of reflecting and focusing on a particular experience, so allowing us to gain new insights'.

Inspired by Campbell (1993) and his theory of a mythical and archetypal hero found in societies throughout the world, Chisholm (2000) extracts metaphorical stages of a journey that can be used as useful signposts for service-learning students. Her book is an essential and core reference textbook for students embarking on international service-learning. It can also be adapted for use with home students to structure their journal writing using selected stages of a metaphorical journey as in a literary 'monomyth'. Chisholm's stages are: 'Hearing the Call'; 'Preparing for the Journey'; 'Departing and Separating'; 'Crossing the First Threshold'; Taking up the Challenges'; 'Battling the Beasts'; 'Passing through the Gates'; 'Recognizing Guides and Guardian Spirits'; 'Celebrating the Victories'; 'Discovering the Boon'; 'Charting the Course', and 'Returning Home' (p. x). A typical journal entry for each stage of a student's metaphorical journey might include a brief description of their service activities; analysis of how their service experience relates to the coursework; and an evaluation of their personal development. Each journal entry could also be structured to represent an experiential learning cycle, as referred to in Chapter 3.

A journal entry model

It is helpful to students to read an example of work that is expected in a written assignment. This is of particular importance when the assignment is unfamiliar to them. Here is an example from my service experiences in Thailand, which I use to demonstrate a journal entry. In class, this passage is scrutinised by students who are asked to identify where its stages of an experiential learning cycle occur, how it relates to a stage in Chisholm's text (2000), and to comment critically on its presentation. I have used this journal entry in class without initially revealing to students my identity as its author. This method usually elicits frank and critical deliberations from students. I later reveal its authorship by showing students photographs taken from my service experience that illustrate the journal entry.

Stage 2: Taking up the challenges

Finally we arrived at the retreat in Thailand. The first task was to make our way to each of our allotted huts. They were individually built and from the outside looked similar to bijou villas with steps leading up to a small veranda and the door. A water tap sprouted from the outside wall and underneath it lay a round metallic bowl. I tentatively climbed the steps up to the villa, opened the door and went inside. It immediately occurred to me that this is how Alice in Wonderland might have felt when she suddenly started to grow big and everything in the room seemed to shrink and appear so small (Carroll, 1993). Before me was a tiny, almost empty, room which was the entire interior space of the villa. A neatly folded blanket lay tucked in one corner. This is where I was to sleep, on the bare floor-boards. There would be just enough room for me to lie down. I was not sure that the next few days were going to be much fun after all. This was the first challenge. I thought about some of my companions who were taller than me and imagined how much more uncomfortable they were going to be in their huts.

As instructed previously, I took off my wristwatch and pieces of jewellery before changing into the thin white cotton baggy trousers and tunic top that had been previously supplied to each of us. The trousers were another challenge: how were they to stay up? The waist was enormous and there were no obvious fasteners, just two very long ties sewn at each side. After puzzling for a while and trying different techniques, I eventually wound the ties round my middle to resemble a kind of ornate celtic knot and resignedly pulled the tunic down to cover it. Dressed thus and barefoot, I was to join a number of Buddhist monks and the rest of my companions for our first meditation session in the Thai retreat. This was only to be an introduction, as tomorrow at 5.30 a.m. we would begin meditation practice that would continue over two days. I shut the door behind me and walked tentatively down the short steps, feeling a little self-conscious and a little forlorn, already missing some of my identity in the heap of clothes and jewellery that I had left lying on the floor of the hut.

In many ways, discarding our Western clothes and personal adornments and replacing them with plain unisex clothing was symbolic. It revealed that ultimately we are all the same: we are all human. It highlighted our attachment to material goods and began to direct our focus to another attachment, the attachment to self and ego. Professional or financial status, gender, class, 'race', age, ability, what type of house you inhabit, what type of car you drive are accessories to, and become mere diversions from, our essential humanity. This moment was a hiatus. It was like having an opportunity to start again, by being shown a different way of thinking and perceiving the world. This was a challenge. I cast my mind back to when I had studied Buddhist philosophy and psychology during my undergraduate years. It had all been theory. This was for real: this was Buddhism in practice (The Dalai Lama, 2002). When one of the monks began to speak to us, fragments of my past learning through Buddhist texts, in particular from the *Abhidammattha Sangaha* (Nārada, 1975), came flooding back. I began to feel more comfortable and more at ease as what he said resonated with my memory of long forgotten ideas. As the ideas returned, connecting the past with the present, I embraced them.

These first two days signalled the beginning of my international service and this experience prepared a more balanced and grounded attitude for a return to life in the West. In retrospect, it became clear that this experience heralded the beginning of personal re-evaluation and redefinition, the implications of which were to continue long after my return to the United Kingdom.

Examples of students' journal entries (from the structure by Chisholm [2000])

Having obtained approval from the ethics committee at the university where I teach and the service-learning students' written informed consent, I have extracted excerpts from a selection of their journals from 2006 to 2013 to demonstrate eight selected stages of a metaphorical hero's journey (Chisholm, 2000). Using different excerpts reveals the uniqueness of students' experience and learning. Pseudonyms are used in the journal entries to protect the anonymity of staff and service-users in the welfare agencies where the students' service-learning placements were hosted. The agencies represent a wide range of services to the community, which may be perceived in each entry. What is presented here is not intended to be read as a continuous narrative as each entry was written by a different student. The extracts represent communal stages of service-learning experience while also revealing the rich diversity of students' reflections.

Hearing the call (Student B)

My journey, which resulted in participating within the service-learning programme, began fifteen years ago when I was seven years old. At that time I viewed the world through the innocent eyes of a child, believing that everyone was as lucky as I, that everyone lived within a stable loving home, within a quaint little village, with the same opportunities available. At that age, I loved school. I enjoyed learning new and exciting facts, and being able to explore my creativity through my schooling. As a little girl who had a passion for learning, it was no surprise that when faced with the question of 'what do you want to do when you grow up?' I announced, 'teach': I associated learning with positive experiences and so wanted to share that joy.

However, during the summer holidays that year, I experienced one of the most distressing events that could happen to a child situated within a happy, stable working class family – my parents separated and later divorced. Along with the departure of my father, my teaching aspirations left, and I became consumed with my own grief and self-pity. Some months later, I was travelling home on the school bus when a girl in my class, who had only recently moved to the school, approached me. She told me that her parents were breaking up, and that she didn't know what to do. I was confused – why was this girl, whom I barely knew, divulging these details to me? I questioned her about this, and she responded, 'Because your parents have split up'. I then realised that despite the heartache I was experiencing, I could use this to ease the pain of someone else, by helping this girl through the same terrible journey that I had recently gone through.

I did not realise it then, but it was at this moment that I heard my true calling: to help others.

Fifteen years later, after commencing and then ending my study in psychology (due to the competitiveness and lack of concentration on my goal of helping others), combined with my interest in the social and political realms of society, I was presented with the unique opportunity to participate within a service-learning programme. The course offered the prospect of experiencing a new culture, witnessing different view and beliefs, and how different individuals' circumstances influence behaviours. It was an opportunity for me to personally 'advance the social good' (Rhoads, 2000, p. 37) through a combination of furthering my education at university, whilst participating in service to the community. My reasons for participating in the course may appear to have been self-interested (Scott and Seglow, 2007), however, it is suggested that reciprocity, situated 'somewhere between pure altruism and pure self-interest' (p. 94), may be an easier way to define an altruistic act, as this suggests that an act remains altruistic if it involves some sort of sacrifice without the reassurance that the sacrifice will be returned. Therefore perhaps this definition more accurately describes my act of participating in the service-learning programme as I was willing to help the agency with whatever was needed, whilst sacrificing my day off, despite being unsure of what I would gain from the experience.

Rhoads's (2000, p. 37) theory of the 'caring self' also resonated with me, in that my aims of helping others were, in my opinion, a result of a genuine 'concern for the well-being of others'. I attempted to go into my service with an open mind and was prepared to have my values and beliefs challenged to enable a deeper level of understanding. Rhoads suggests that to achieve a democratic society, the caring self must be promoted, through mutuality (the sharing of thoughts and ideas), personalisation meaning interacting with others, and reflection on experience to identify deeper meanings, which I was able to do through my service and through my interaction within seminars with other service-learning students. Therefore, after hearing the call all those years ago, the service-learning course presented the ideal opportunity for me to create and achieve my caring self, whilst fulfilling my call of helping others. Hearing the call marked the beginning of my long and sometimes arduous journey through service to where I am today.

Taking up the challenges (Student C)

At first I struggled to link my reflections with a wider meaning of the outside world. They all seemed to be concentrated on processes inside myself that were allowing for a lot of self-discovery but little revelation about the world around me. One book chapter that helped me in particular with this task was 'Liberation through Consciousness Raising' (Hart, 1990). One sentence in this chapter suddenly made everything clear, '[P]ersonal experience can only be the necessary *point of departure* for gaining socially valid knowledge, it cannot itself constitute the whole universe of such knowledge' (p. 67). After reading this, something just clicked into place and I could recognise all the processes that were taking place. Hart's description of the cycle of consciousness raising (pp. 70–1) allowed me to identify and clarify what I was doing and it all became much easier after that. I did not go into my voluntary agency with an open mind. I have realised now that the fear of not having an open mind had actually closed my mind. I had never worked with elderly or disabled people before and so was very nervous about this. I was so worried that they would think that I was not treating them 'normally'. I was so scared of seeming ageist or patronising. In worrying about how I would treat the service-users, I was treating them differently than I would treat other people and so, without realising it, was doing the exact thing that I was trying to avoid, being discriminatory. My fear of seeming rude paralysed me, and I did not engage fully with any of the service-users as I was too aware of how I was behaving towards them. Reflecting on my behaviour and asking why I felt like this allowed me to realise I was being discriminatory. As a result I vowed to change. The next week, because I was aware of my previous mistake, I threw myself into interacting with the service-users, and it was not until the end of the day that I became conscious of the fact that I had not once thought about how I was treating the service-users. This is because I had dropped my inhibitions and prejudices and was simply treating them as if they were any other new acquaintance, which is of course exactly what they were. This was first experience of how critical thought and reflection changed my actions, as it is meant to, in Kolb's (1984) experiential learning cycle.

Battling the beasts (Student D)

I sat among the other workers and chatted for a while in between writing up the survey. Everything was relaxed and I felt welcomed. Then Jane walked into the room. Jane rents a desk in the office for her work as a training co-ordinator in the city. I know her though my mum, who had worked with her previously and developed a close friendship. Jane said hello to me very informally. I answered her with the same ease and informality that she used to ask the questions. I could see the girls around me were taken aback by the fact that I knew Jane and by the informal tone of our conversation. When she left the room, Jennifer enquired as to how I knew Jane. I told her, and from that moment I noticed strangeness in her voice. She was almost accusing in her tone, questioning how much I actually knew about the type of service the agency was engaged in and how much experience I had in the area. I don't have experience in the area, not practical real experience, just theoretical and academic understanding and I have always tried to convey that I realise this doesn't compare to practical experience.

Jennifer was clearly not convinced of my lack of understanding or knowledge. The phone rang at my desk, and I looked at the other girls to come and answer it. Jennifer told me to answer it. I knew she was testing me. In another situation I wouldn't have risen to the challenge because I didn't feel adequately trained to respond to a user of this service. The phone continued to ring and as Jennifer's test rang in my ears, I panicked.

I answered the phone. A woman with a quiet timid voice began to tell me of her experience and asked for advice or support available through the agency. I was completely unprepared to answer this call, but attempted to put my anger at Jennifer aside in order to show support and sympathy. I came off the phone and looked to Jennifer for an apology for putting me in that position. The apology never came, neither did the thank you. Anger pushed me out of the room and to the bathroom. Tears began to boil up behind my eyes, trying to spill out onto the hot surface of my cheek. I tried desperately to cool down the heat inside of me and push the tears down to simmer, for now. I walked back into the room and worked quietly until it was time to finish, time to go home where I could let my emotions out in private. I could cry and not know exactly why I was crying. I could be angry and not know exactly who I was angry at. I just needed the privacy to reflect on what had happened and regain my composure in order to understand the best thing to do. bell hooks's account of the notion of internalised racism in *Black Beauty and Black Power* provoked me to reconsider what the real beast was in this critical incident that I had encountered in my placement. hooks (1995, p. 119) argues that 'white supremacy had assaulted our self-concept and our self-esteem'. This analysis of white supremacy and the impact that colonisation has had on creating the standards of beauty within the black community, led me to apply this concept to the situation with Jennifer. We live under male supremacy in a patriarchal society; therefore women inevitably internalise this oppression.

It is easy to name the beast and to personify this mythical creature that must be slain. However, applying the theoretical concepts of hooks to the situation forms a new understanding of what the beast really is and what the best way is to deal with it. If patriarchy has impacted on women in the same way that white supremacy has impacted on people of colour, then both Jennifer and I have experienced an assault on our self-concept and our self-esteem. Therefore, it appears understandable that in situations where we feel inadequate, inferior, or questioned in our roles, we will retaliate not at a wider political level of challenging patriarchy, but towards those around us, consequently exemplifying Freire's (1970, p. 45) theory that the oppressed, in their quest for power, often take on the role of the 'sub-oppressor'. As I reflected in my journal about the beast that I had encountered, I realised that this beast was not Jennifer.

This new understanding of internalised oppression helped me to recognise the true beast. This recognition 'granted me the serenity to accept the things I cannot change', that patriarchy has led to an internalisation of female oppression; 'gave me courage to change the things I can', the way that I deal with the situation can now be objective and not retaliating by attempting to take on the oppressive role myself; and 'wisdom to know the difference', which is necessary in all critical incidents to know the right action to take in response to the specific situation. With this understanding, my actions towards the situation changed. I composed an objective email to the manager of the agency explaining the incident and asked for adequate training in answering the phone. This training was given to me the next day I went to the agency, giving me confidence to deal with any further situations that arose.

Passing through the gates (Student E)

Throughout my childhood, community was something viewed from a distance. Community was what existed outside of the home, divided into sections independent of one another. Society was neatly segmented, compartmentalised according to the class in which you were born and in which you were expected to stay. Problems belonged in the private realm and help and support sought within the family or from close friends. Support for others could be offered without direct contact, for example, by donation to charity. However, Dewey's perception of democratic society in action is: 'a way of relational living in which the decisions and actions of one citizen must be understood in terms of their influence on the lives of others' (Rhoads in Baxter, 2000, p. 28). This illustrates for me that democracy is not simply a political system but a complex human process. Service has not only heightened my awareness of others' needs, rights, and difference but it has also given me a sense of location within this process. When I leave the agency, the actions I choose to take will continue to impact on others, just as others' actions affect me.

My parents, with the best will in the world, discouraged me from entering 'stressful' professions such as social work, where the messy problems of others' lives could upset the equilibrium of my own. Yet if I see myself as being part of democratic society in Dewey's terms, I feel a responsibility to use the skills and knowledge I have gained to help others, just as I have been helped. I am also reminded of Putnam's (1995, p. 67) concepts of social capital and social trust, and his suggestion that 'networks of interaction probably broaden the participants' sense of self, developing the "I" into "we"'.

Rhoads sums up the value of service-learning as giving students an opportunity to see how 'their personal worlds intersect with the worlds of others' (Rhoads in Baxter, 2000, p. 43) and my time at the agency helps me to do this: to see the diversity that exists in the community, and to define more distinctly my own place within it, both personally and in career choices I feel I will now make.

Recognising guides and guardian spirits (Student F)

> In service-learning, those being served control the service provided.
>
> Jacoby, 1996, p. 7

Throughout my eight weeks on placement I was helped by all the staff, but particularly by Sheila. It took me a while to notice but she consistently asked me about the work that I was carrying out as a way of getting me to think about and assess my role as part of the organisation and how I was being perceived by clients. Often this called for me to re-evaluate my approach and my perception through critical reflection. This has been important as I have learned to now ask myself these questions as a self-assessment and this will a good exercise to practice as I undertake new projects in the future.

However, I was, somewhat shamefully, surprised that the clients themselves were the main source of encouragement and reassurance for my efforts to help them. By thanking me for making something more easily understood, or telling me what they wanted me to help them with, they were giving me indications of the direction I should be taking, ensuring that I was working with them in order to help them. Looking back, it would seem obvious that they should be the ones to guide me, since they were the reason for my being there. In realisation of this, I overcame an 'epistemic distortion' (Mezirow, 1990) or 'epistemological assumption', a form of pre-reflective thinking that knowledge is true if it comes from an authority figure (King, 2000). In this context, I was originally inclined to believe that I should always go with what the staff advised me to do and whilst they were successful in helping clients into the workplace, it did not mean that they were owners of true knowledge or had all the answers.

In recognising the guidance from service-users, I was led to critically assess my role and position at the agency. The change from my looking for direction from staff to seek evaluation and input from the service-users seemingly corresponds to much of Freire's (1970) work on 'conscientisation' and the recognition of sources of oppression. I considered if I was in fact furthering the oppression of the service-users by conforming to a potential power imbalance between them and the staff. Given the fact that I was helping to deliver some of the courses, it was easy to see my role as a teaching assistant, which created a teacher-student dynamic. Being aware of this though, I tried my best to overcome this by adjusting my behaviour and even what I was wearing in order to feel more level with the service-users.

Also, Blackburn (2000) states that here are assumptions underpinning Freirean pedagogy, including the assumption that an oppressed group has no power at all, and in truth, the aim of the course was to empower service-users to overcome cultural and language barriers as well as prejudice by giving them the knowledge and confidence to deal with them. In accepting help from guides, Chisholm (2000) highlighted that there are qualities we must possess in order to be offered guidance. Humility played a hugely important role in my being able to relate to the service-users, by showing sensitivity towards them. I learned through experience how this benefited our relationship and so will remember its importance when I am working with others, particularly for any future work that I do with more vulnerable individuals.

Celebrating the victories (Student G)

> Reaching conclusions too quickly is dangerous for those in a new situation. One often hears people who have but a brief encounter speaking authoritatively, as if they were experts on that culture.
> (Chisholm, 2000, p. 211)

For me, this quote sums up some of the predicaments in evaluating my time in service-learning. Having reflected on empirical evidence as to accepted practice in the agency and its activities, I have been aware only of my own responses to this and I did not feel it my place to take great consultation with staff on many of the larger issues on which I have written and at times I have been aware that the word 'journal' as an academic result may have provoked a feeling that I was auditing. To this extent, I still feel that to speak in broad brushstrokes is problematic, considering that the agency has been in existence for over fifteen years, myself having spent eight weeks there. Indeed, I wonder if perhaps I should be reserving judgement about the agency itself, given that the experiences I've had and the coursework begs to increase our awareness of suspending judgement and taking time to evaluate.

Due to this, and some of the contrasts in my experience, I have decided to return – something which I actually consider a major victory; that I have been permitted and encouraged to go back. Many of the biggest achievements I have already outlined, in particular, overcoming some of the barriers of conversation. This occurred elsewhere when a service-user requested something of me from the café area, and it was only upon reflection that I realised I had understood immediately what was being asked, and that clearly I had become accustomed to his speech patterns.

Smaller victories however have been important to me and once more they have been in the form of subtle recognitions. For example, a group of service-users came to associate me with a particular activity which I sometimes joined them in, and I was often asked if I would be participating from week to week. In other activities such as the women's confidence building and self defence classes, I sharpened my skills of engagement and interaction. In one particular session, I found myself anxious that issues of security and protection were not being linked with larger issues of violence against women and sexism. However, I was aware that the group session was not *for* my voice, and it may have been unnecessary to scare people by highlighting dangers so early on in the programme, and indeed these group meetings did later take on a 'mutually self reflective' element (Hart, 1990). Moreover, I realised that my passion for this topic was no good without the ability to see and truly listen to other points of view or to conceptualise why certain elements were not dealt with immediately.

Discovering the boon (Student H)

Such critical thinking has permitted me to see myself and the wider world in new and transforming ways and is something that I believe I have discovered through a series of thoughts and events. There is not any one situation in particular that has encouraged me to continue my journey to parts unknown as a result of critical thinking; rather it has been a number of collective experiences which have allowed me to appreciate my own purpose and limitations. At the climax of my journey I have stumbled upon what I consider to be the true purpose of the service-learning programme. That is, the realisation and discovery of my enhanced critical awareness which has in fact supported and assisted me throughout my time at my agency, allowing me to question not only my own assumptions, but those of service-users and service providers.

The discovery of such a boon has encouraged personal growth and maturity and has taught me to question my assumptions and perspectives, not only towards the issues in my agency, but towards aspects of wider society. Throughout my journey it has nurtured my critical thinking and critical reflection in preparation for a heightened awareness of the existing oppression within my agency and the courses from which such oppression stems. I began to make clear and concise connections to the structure of oppression in my agency, and as I think back to my first day, I remember the thoughts and assumptions I held and how they have changed. The realisation that the service-learning had given me the opportunity to view such instances with greater understanding and increased critical awareness has benefited me no end. I am more conscious of the significance of service-learning and the impact it has had on my journey which is nearing its completion, without which I imagine I would have remained somewhat ignorant. Such heightened critical awareness has allowed me to expand my capacity for critical thinking and critical reflection and is consequential of the application of praxis as a learning technique (Dewey, 1938). According to Freire (1970), such awareness is rooted in critical reflection and collective struggle rather than indoctrination and, contends Blackburn (2000), is the first step in the pursuit for greater humanisation. This text links directly to the service-learning programme I have experienced and demonstrates the pathway in which I have been following in my realisation that my quest should benefit the oppressed and the greater good.

The gradual unearthing and recognition of my critical consciousness has encouraged me to critically question situations or incidents that I may have once made assumptions about or passed judgement on. Coupled with critical reflection, this heightened awareness has allowed me to perceive things from different perspectives before reaching a conclusion and – through the process of praxis which lies at the heart of service-learning – has reinforced my desire and ambition to make a difference in the lives of the societies disadvantaged, vulnerable, and oppressed.

Charting the course (Student I)

As this journey came to a close, I began to reflect on the lessons that I can take from my experience of service-learning. I have learned how to better interpret my actions, and the actions of others, in order to identify underlying assumptions. I have learned how to extrapolate meaning and value from a seemingly negative situation. I have developed a stronger sense of self and purpose recognising that 'it is impossible for the self to develop outside of social experience' (Rhoads, 2000, p. 40). Through engaging with other people I have learned much about the person that I am. I have learned how to connect my experiences of citizenship and participation with the wider world.

Deeley (2004, p. 197) argues that 'deep learning occurs when concepts are directly related to experience'. I find myself relating to this idea as I feel that I will carry the lessons that I have learned beyond this course. Lessons such as these, in my experience, are not possible within a traditional framework of education. Dewey (1938, pp. 18–19) argues that progressive education promotes 'development from within' whilst traditional education tries to instil 'formation from without'. As I leave the traditional framework of education, of which I have been part for 17 years, I carry into the outside world important tools with which to continue my life-long learning. This has given me a sense of peace about leaving university and also a hope for what I can go on to achieve. As Illich (1971, p. 39) says, '[M]ost learning is not the result of instruction. It is rather the result of unhampered participation in a meaningful setting'.

If I truly want 'to save the world', then I must continue to reflect and challenge the assumptions and oppressive structures that I see. My experiences can and will inform this as I recognise that 'the private is the political' (Hart, 1990, p. 49). Linked to this, I have an increased sense of career direction. For me, I have found that service-learning has further increased my sense of social responsibility and nourished confidence in my ability to make a difference in society (Daigre, 2000, p. 14).

'Thus one journeyed, returning finally to the kingdom where the road began. But one was not the same, nor was the kingdom' (Chisholm, 2000, p. 5). Interestingly enough, this journey ended where it began. I've explored my childhood passions, challenged my teenage pursuits, and focused my adult ambition. I took my values and preconceptions into the real world and along the way they were challenged, revitalised, and restored. But the journey is not over.

Learning

In service-learning, assessment is a function of and justification for academic writing within journals. From this perspective, journals are products of learning. Nevertheless, journal writing is also a 'vehicle' for student learning (Boud, 2001, p. 9) and, therefore, can be perceived as a process (Mannion, 2001). Through the use of journal writing, students can become more active in their learning as they endeavour to make meaning from their service and academic coursework combined. Kerka (2002, p. 1) eloquently explains that 'a journal is a crucible for processing the raw material of experience in order to integrate it with existing knowledge and create new meaning'. Critical reflection is an essential component of journal writing and is 'a process of turning experience into learning, that is, a way of exploring experience in order to learn new things from it' (Boud, 2001, p. 10). In this sense, journal writing may follow the same pattern as an experiential learning cycle, which requires reflecting on and re-evaluating past events for learning that will inform future action. As such, this method of writing can help to overcome 'cognitive dissonance' (Moon, 2006, p. 25) where there is tension between students' prior and new knowledge, through a process of assimilation and understanding.

Reflective writing is essential to journals and serves 'to enhance creative and critical thinking' (Thorpe, 2004, p. 328). Critical awareness of events and the coursework theory are both needed for students to be able to reflect meaningfully in service-learning as knowledge is required to make sense of the ill-structured events that constitute data for the journals. Students must then be able to communicate effectively through the structure of the journal. Journal writing may also help students to perceive changes in their perspective (Jarvis, 2001) and thus can be 'liberating' (Mannion, 2001, p. 97). From a social constructivist perspective this process may be referred to as 'building own personal theory' (Moon, 2006, p. 96). Here, '[m]eaning is relational: it relates to a whole chain of language (and is) linguistically contextual' (Mannion, 2001, p. 104). Consequently, active and deep learning can occur, which may generate a sense of students' 'ownership' of their learning. This is generated from students' critical reflection on their own experiences and from challenging assumptions which is 'central to understanding how adults learn to think for themselves rather than act on the concepts, values, and feelings of others' (Mezirow, 1998, p. 185). Service-learning can offer students this opportunity which can lead them to the road of critical action that points in the direction of critical being, or becoming. Such is the holistic element within service-learning. Inherently, personal and emotive factors are part of this as they play essential roles in this type of learning (Moon, 2006) and its expression through personal narrative in journal writing.

Journal writing also encourages metacognition, which is a skill whereby students become aware of how they learn, widening and deepening their overall intellectual development. Journal writing is appropriate within service-learning because it acts as the final conduit between service and learning, providing evidence of students' critical reflections. As such, journal writing is 'an invaluable tool that can lead to personal ... enrichment and empowerment' (Jarvis, 2001, p. 85). This is reinforced by Hiemstra (2001) who claims that journal writing has several benefits, including advancing personal development and self-expression, as well as increased skills in critical thinking and reflection. In addition to theoretical analysis, journal writing in service-learning inevitably involves the self and personal experience. As a method of learning, journal writing is very useful and gives service-learning students a medium through which to demonstrate their critical reflection on their service experience and coursework study. Journal writing, however, is not all 'a bed of roses'. There may be obstacles in students' understanding of what is expected from them in terms of this type of academic writing. It is therefore imperative that clear guidelines and opportunities to practice writing are given to students before they submit a formal reflective journal for summative assessment. Furthermore, some students may also be apprehensive about writing from a personal perspective and this may inhibit their writing skills.

Assessment

It is valuable to students' learning to engage in and receive feedback on formative assessment (Deeley, 2014; Jessop et al., 2012; Jarvis, 2010; Nicol and McFarlane-Dick, 2006). As part of their learning, service-learning students may keep fieldwork notes in a personal or 'working' journal for their private use. It is from this that they can extract relevant data to write a formal journal for summative assessment. This strategy lessens any potentially controversial dilemma that might arise (Moon, 2006) or ethical risk of inappropriate personal disclosure because students can filter the data collection before writing their formal journal.

As stated earlier, journals are evidence of a process as well as being a product. What this means is that within the journal entries there should be evidence of the process of a student's critical thinking using their practical service experiences to demonstrate examples and using the academic coursework to provide support for their argument. It is the quality and depth of critical reflection which can be assessed (Kember et al., 1999). Within their journals, it is important for students to demonstrate what and how they have learned by relating the theoretical aspects of the coursework to their service experience, as well as analysing and commenting critically on the relevance of theory for their future action or practice. The criteria for assessment of the journals can be either pre-set or generated collaboratively between the teacher and students (Heron, 1988). Kember et al. (1999) developed criteria for assessing reflective thinking which could be used as a guide to inform journal marking to differentiate between non-reflective, habitual, thoughtful, and reflective action. If students are involved in the design of marking criteria for their journals, this collaboration may further enhance a sense of ownership of their learning. An example of journal marking criteria that I have used previously in my course with some brief explanatory guidance to students is presented here.

Extent to which the aim of the journal has been addressed

The aim is to reflect critically on your experiences in your community service and to make critical connections with the academic content of the course. The content of the journal should meet the aims and intended learning outcomes of the course.

Clarity, structure, and presentation

There should be a structural progression through various stages of a metaphorical journey (Chisholm, 2000), details of which will be discussed in class. You should write clearly and to an accepted academic standard. There should be clarity and good observation of events and issues.

Evidence of reflective thinking

There should be evidence of action/reflection compatible with an experiential learning cycle (Beard and Wilson, 2002, p. 29). There should be evidence of critical awareness, an honest approach to self-assessment, and a willingness to revise ideas. The reflective aspects of the journal should be in depth, preferably noting questions or issues that arise from the reflective process and on which further reflection may be made.

Development of critical analysis

There should be a demonstration of critical analysis that relates the academic course content with your experiential learning. There should be evidence of your cognitive skills, for example, comprehension, analysis, synthesis, and evaluation.

Evidence of reading

Critical reading of the relevant literature should be evident throughout the journal in your critical analysis and structure, that is, stages of a metaphorical journey. There should be a clear relationship between the journal entries and specific, relevant coursework and theories.

Referencing and bibliography

Using the Harvard system of referencing, this is the same as for essay writing.

Conclusion

This chapter aimed to examine academic writing in service-learning because it is different from what is expected in conventional assignments in higher education. Service-learning demands a different approach to assessment because of its experiential learning framework. Learning is personalised and depends on individual experience and the making sense of unique and often ill-structured experiences while on service placement. To bridge the gap between theory and practice, it is vital for students to engage in critical reflection. This is a learning process undertaken in structured tutorial class discussions and a skill matured epigenetically with practice through students' writing exercises. These exercises, or assignments, are therefore a process in the students' learning and also serve as a product of their learning that can be assessed. The written assessments used in my service-learning courses have been presented as examples, but there may be other effective methods of assessment.

Writing critical incidents is a very useful method of learning to think reflectively and critically. It demands a halt to the constant mental traffic of information and causes students to explore in small structured steps the reflective process through a series of simple questions. Analysis, evaluation, criticality, and reflexivity can be demonstrated and assessed through the writing of critical incidents and therefore present a useful contribution to assessment within service-learning.

Similarly, journal writing involves the process of critical reflection, analysis, evaluation, and reflexivity but in more depth and more detail. Students need to think critically in order to relate the abstract conceptualisations within, and the theoretical aspects of, the coursework to their practical experiences of service in the community. Writing journals involves, therefore, reflective practice and, as such, is a process. In their journals, students demonstrate this critical and reflective practice, drawing on their service experiences and analysing relevant coursework theory to substantiate their argument. As such, journals are products and can thus be assessed.

The content of students' journals is grounded in their own experience, which allows them to take ownership of their learning and understanding. The journals are written to an accepted academic standard and an autobiographical narrative is used through storytelling and metaphorical allusions. Using the idea of an eponymous hero on an adventurous journey to the unknown and unfamiliar, students can apply their autobiographical experiences under a cloak of anonymity. As personal experience and self-reflection are intrinsic to service-learning journals, the use of metaphors in discourse is ideal. Metaphors are used to communicate experiences that are sensitive, subjective, and complex (Semino, 2014). By providing the steps, signposts, or stages of a metaphorical journey (Chisholm, 2000), students are enabled to relate their experiences and learning in a structured and logical manner.

There may be some initial resistance to this format as it is an innovative method of assessment in higher education with which students may be unfamiliar. Nevertheless, as evidence from students reveals in the next chapter, this type of assessment is appropriately conducive to achieving deep learning. Academic writing in this style and using metaphors, offers an opportunity to connect theory with practice and attempts to reconcile the 'personal with the political'. This gives students a sense of structure and objectivity that allows them to reflect critically.

Academic writing in service-learning, therefore, offers students and teachers the opportunity to step outside the traditional boundaries and methods of learning and assessment. The examples in this chapter of writing critical incidents and reflective journals are not exclusive to service-learning, nor are they the only choice of assignments available and appropriate to service-learning. A critical choice must be taken that is consistent with the alignment of assessment with the aims and intended learning outcomes of any course (Biggs and Tang, 2011). The efficacy of assessment involving critical incidents and reflective journals in service-learning is the focus of the next chapter, which is grounded on empirical evidence from my research study in which service-learning students reflected in and on assessment.

7
Reflections in and on Assessment

Introduction

Following the previous chapter on academic writing in service-learning, this chapter examines what students themselves think about assessment in service-learning. In order to do this, empirical evidence from my pedagogical research presents students' reflections in and on their service-learning assessment. The assessment is outlined and explained, with particular attention paid to innovative summative co-assessment methods (Deeley, 2014) that are transferable to other academic courses and may contribute not only to the enhancement of students' employability skills, competencies, and graduate attributes, but also to deep and lifelong learning.

It could be argued that traditional means of assessment, in particular unseen examinations, are incompatible with the active and experiential learning intrinsic to this type of course and that non-traditional assessment methods are more appropriate to service-learning. As service-learning students must reflect critically on their academic coursework and practical experience, it is appropriate that their assessment is aligned to this and allows them to demonstrate their critical reflections and analysis. This chapter focuses on students' reflections within their assignments and on the assessment methods. Overall, my qualitative research study reveals that students' critical capabilities can be developed, as well as appraised, through assessment.

Firstly, however, a review of relevant literature is undertaken in order to have a wider view of assessment before focusing on particular assessment methods for service-learning. This review concerns the relevance of using formative assessment as assessment for learning by giving appropriate feedback, especially if the method of assessment is new to the students. The value of summative assessment as assessment of learning is discussed, with the perspective that it is also useful for learning if feedback is given.

Traditional assessment usually involves a top-down system that is often shrouded in mystique to students not initiated into its processes. Consequently, students commonly play a passive role in assessment. The method of co-assessment challenges this approach because it can involve collaboration between staff and students, or between students and their peers, in assessment activities and processes. The benefits and challenges of collaborative assessment are scrutinised in this chapter.

After an overview and discussion of assessment in theory, the practical effects on students are examined. I undertook an investigation in to the efficacy and effectiveness of non-traditional forms of assessment in service-learning through a practitioner research study. Insightful findings emerged through the scrutiny of students' reflections on their assessment, which are discussed in this chapter. The conclusions reached are from a small scale investigation, nevertheless, they indicate that the non-traditional assessment methods used are conducive to enhancing students' critical thinking skills and there is some evidence to support the view that service-learning may indeed be perceived as a critical pedagogy.

Assessment

Assessment is a necessary part of, and intrinsic to, higher education. It serves to develop and reinforce learning in addition to being a measure or judgement of the learning that has occurred. Assessment can be seen as a process (Race, 2001) which is an inevitable and inherent part of academic courses. It can be used summatively to measure or judge whether and to what extent learning has taken place, and formatively, to enhance student learning. Summative assessment is often regarded as assessment of learning, whereas formative assessment is for learning, where feedback plays a vital role in students' development. The aim of summative assessment is to indicate the extent to which learning has occurred and is therefore the tool with which to grade students' coursework, allow student progression, and award degree classifications. It is important to note, however, that summative assessment can also be used to enhance student learning.

Formative assessment, by contrast, is often used diagnostically (Jarvis, 2010) so that weaknesses or gaps within a student's learning may be revealed and subsequently addressed. This is useful because it may take account of slow learners or it can be useful as 'practice', especially when a new method of assessment is being implemented. Formative assessment is therefore a pivotal and critical point in the process of learning (Jessop et al., 2012).

Assessment can encourage learning because it can create extrinsic motivation, in that students need to learn in order to pass examinations and thus attain qualifications. There is a downside to this, however, because assessment can reinforce strategic and surface learning, such as '"swotting for exams" rather than trying to internalise and make sense of the subject' (Boud, 1990, p. 104). Alternatively, assessment can enhance learning by inspiring intrinsic motivation where students have a desire to learn. As Boud explains, 'Meaningful learning is more likely to occur when students engage with the subject matter for its own sake, not for that of an extrinsic demand' (p. 102). Assessment can influence students' confidence and affect the type of learning that occurs (Boud and Falchikov, 2007; Knight and Yorke, 2003; McMahon, 1999). Through different types of assessment, students can learn how to learn and have the means to know that they have learned (Heron, 1988). This metacognitive skill can be developed in service-learning through assessment which involves the application of critical reflection and its ensuing analysis and evaluation.

Different types of assessment may be used specifically at different times in an academic course. To illustrate this, the aim of formative assessment, with the use of constructive feedback is to improve learning and naturally would be placed early in a course of study. Another example is ipsative assessment, which is a further development of formative assessment that 'compares existing performance with previous performance' (Hughes, 2011, p. 353). By contrast, summative assessment is usually employed as a measurement or judgement of learning that primarily aims to provide a statement of achievement and, as such, would normally be placed at the end of a course of study, although summatively assessed coursework can be situated at different times throughout a course, which is useful to enhance student learning.

Assessment may be perceived as an exact measurement of learning, but in some circumstances it is more appropriately a judgement. In discursive subjects, for example, within the arts, humanities, and social sciences, there may not always be a correct or incorrect answer. As judgement, it can be argued that assessment is mostly subjective (Hughes, 2011), which raises the issue of its reliability and the extent to which it is possible for assessors to be objective or consistently objective (Yorke, 2011). Whether assessment is summative or formative, it is essential that accuracy, fairness, and consistency are evident. Other important factors include the validity, authenticity, transparency, effectiveness, and credibility of assessment (Bloxham and Boyd, 2007; Knight, 2002; Gray, 2001; Race, 2001). It is also important that course assessment is aligned to its intended learning outcomes or objectives and that the criteria for marking reflects this (Rust, 2007; Pickford and Brown, 2006; Biggs, 2003).

Feedback

Effective and timely feedback on coursework is most helpful for students' learning (Price et al., 2010; Sadler, 2010). Feedback can be written or oral, but it generally contains a message to students about what they did well in their assignment and what could be improved. Reference to the extent to which intended learning outcomes were achieved and the marking criteria were met can be helpful. Constructive feedback is an essential aspect of assessment and can contribute to the development of effective learning. Unfortunately, feedback can also have negative effects on students' learning. Ill-constructed feedback, for example, can have counter effects on students to the extent that they can be disheartened from continuing with their studies. By contrast, feedback that explains how their work could be improved can encourage students to progress. Feedback is therefore a vital aspect of formative assessment and can facilitate learning (Nicol and McFarlane-Dick, 2006). Indeed, as Taras (2003, p. 549) asserts, feedback is 'unequivocally considered central to learning'. Good feedback practice encourages students to reflect on their learning and make judgements about their own work (Nicol and McFarlane-Dick, 2006). Self-assessment is a useful process for learning and can be highly effective when it is used in conjunction with others' assessment, for example, in co-assessment. During co-assessment, students self-assess which necessitates reflection on their learning. In addition, students are also assessed by their peers or by the teacher. In either case, students receive feedback which they can then compare with their own self-assessment.

Self-assessment

Self-assessment involves students' reflective evaluation and judgement of their own learning (Dochy et al., 1999). There are valuable skills involved in, and developed through, self-assessment (Deeley, 2014), especially critical thinking. The benefits of self-assessment include skills for professional development, confidence, increased awareness, self-reflection, and independent learning (Knight and Yorke, 2003). Monitoring their own performance can give students confidence in their learning and can encourage them to take more responsibility for their learning.

Through the process of self-assessment, students can learn to identify and understand what constitutes excellent work and to apply these standards to their own academic endeavours. A further development from this is for students to engage actively in decisions concerning what is to be assessed and in the generation of criteria or standards to be used in assessment. Nicol and McFarlane-Dick (2006) recommend that students be involved in these matters because student participation encourages deeper learning. It also helps students to be able to define quality work. Self-assessment, therefore, is empowering (Tan, 2007; Falchikov, 2005; Taras, 2003). Furthermore, creating criteria for assessment allows greater transparency in what is to be learned. This is conducive to students being more aware of, and engaged in, their learning and, therefore, encourages student motivation (Stefani, 1994). Self-assessment, therefore, is intrinsic to deep learning (Falchikov, 2005; Race, 2001; Brew, 1999). Self-assessment may be perceived, however, as unreliable and thus belonging only within formative assessment (Stefani, 1994). Nevertheless, reliability in self-assessment appears to improve when feedback is given (Dochy et al., 1999) and where there has been practice in self-assessment. To strengthen the reliability of self-assessment and to provide feedback, co-assessment, in the form of collaboration between the teacher and students, is useful. As Boud (1990, p. 110) asserts, 'Self-assessment in isolation is probably not a fruitful path to follow, but when moderated and used as an element of collaborative assessment its potential is great'.

Co-assessment

Co-assessment is undertaken by different groups who collaborate or work co-operatively together in the assessment process, for example, students and teachers, or students and their peers. It is an effective system because it involves self-assessment and assessment by another, or others. It helps students to develop their skills of self-assessment because they receive feedback both on their work and on the accuracy of their judgement from an external and arguably more objective source, for example, the teacher. Co-assessment is also claimed to enhance learning (Deeley, 2014; Knight and Yorke, 2003).

Co-assessment can be used in different ways, for example, Heron (1988) defines strong and weak models of collaborative assessment. In the strong model the learner and teacher create and agree criteria to be used for assessment, whereas in the weak model the criteria are already established.

The value of co-assessment is mostly perceived in terms of formative assessment and there is scant evidence in the literature which endorses it as part of summative assessment. Nevertheless there is evidence to suggest that it is a reliable and valid form of summative assessment (Deeley, 2014) that captures the vital factors of objectivity and integrity. For summative co-assessment to work effectively where there is collaboration between staff and students, however, it is imperative that there is a trusting relationship between them for the devolved power within the classroom to function. Unfortunately, '[m]any lecturers/tutors express great fear of handing over the power of assessment over to students' (Stefani, 1994, p. 74). There are potential risks involved in striving for a more democratic classroom (Shor, 1987). In doing this, the teacher has less control over learning and teaching which can be unsettling and may give rise to anxiety.

In co-assessment, fear may be rooted in the perceived consequences of vastly different opinions between student and teacher, which could lead to difficult negotiations. Despite this 'risky business' (Deeley, 2014, p. 48) co-assessment can serve to enhance students' skills. It also brings in to focus the political underbelly of educational processes. To reinforce this latter point, Heron (1988,

p. 81) states that '[t]he unilateral model of control and assessment in education is a form of political exploitation, of oppression by professionalism'. Co-assessment counteracts this model and moves towards a democratic approach in learning and teaching. Shrewdly, Creme (2005, p. 289) highlights a common belief that 'we should assess what we have decided is pedagogically important, and that how and what we assess is a powerful influence on student learning'. Co-assessment, however, involves sharing the responsibility of judgement with students, which can be empowering and intrinsically motivating for them. It is also pertinent to note that 'imaginative approaches to assessing skills and practice may significantly impact upon student engagement and achievement' (Pickford and Brown, 2006, p. 124). As such, it is not surprising that the innovative use of co-assessment can result in deep learning. An example of co-assessment, which is relevant to the research study disseminated later in this chapter, concerns students' summatively co-assessed oral presentations where students self-assess the content and delivery of their own presentations and receive feedback from the teacher before agreeing an appropriate mark. In oral presentations, specific subject knowledge as well as communication skills can be assessed.

Co-assessment heralds a move towards a more democratic approach in learning and teaching that enhances deep learning through students' active participation. It nurtures their engagement as autonomous learners and can enhance the development of their employability skills and graduate attributes (Deeley, 2014).

Nevertheless, there is a dearth of studies that investigate effective measures of co-assessment and what students 'actually do, think and feel when they are asked to self-assess...as more evidence of how students perceive of and use self-assessment is needed' (Andrade and Du, 2007, p. 162). What follows is a pedagogical research study on service-learning assessment to investigate students' critical reflections within and on their own academic writing and assessment.

The study

Context

Service-learning is offered as an optional course for third and fourth year Public Policy Honours students in the curriculum of a MA

Social Sciences undergraduate degree in a Scottish university. The academic work in this particular service-learning course is based on the themes of education for citizenship and active citizenship. The 'Education for Citizenship' course is taught in the first semester of an academic year and is followed in the second semester by the 'Active Citizenship' course. 'Education for Citizenship' is theory based, whereas the main focus in 'Active Citizenship' concerns students' service to the community in addition to their critical reflections on how this relates to the theoretical aspects of citizenship studied in the previous semester. Students are required to participate in voluntary work for a period of eight weeks within the semester and for a minimum of six hours each week.

In 2011, service-learning students' reflections within and on their coursework and assessment were investigated. The overarching purpose of this research study was to investigate the effectiveness and effects of non-traditional assessment methods on students in this service-learning course. The assessment included a 5,000-word reflective journal which was weighted at 80% of the overall course grade. In this journal, students were required to demonstrate their service-learning by means of structuring a metaphorical journey in which they interrelated their voluntary work placement experiences with the academic coursework on citizenship. The remaining 20% of the course grade was distributed equally between two other assignments: a critical incident report, as referred to in the previous chapter, and an oral presentation. All of these types of assessment were new to the students, and therefore it was imperative that they fully understood the methods involved (Price et al., 2010). They were given full written and verbal explanations and guidance on the process. In addition, students engaged in formative assessment so that they could familiarise themselves with, and learn from, these new forms of assessment.

With regard to preparation for writing the reflective journal, students kept a personal journal for their notes and reflections in order for them to accumulate progressively the necessary data for the journal. The aim was to record their service activities to give them an opportunity for thoughtful analysis of their experiences. Students were advised to keep a double entry journal, with entries being made initially on the right hand page at least on a weekly basis and ideally on the same day as and soon after their service. Students were encouraged to read their journal entries regularly for further reflections, from which they could then make entries on the left hand page. The content of these later entries could include critical comments or raise issues that relate directly to the course content. In the light of this, students were encouraged to write notes in their personal journals during tutorials as this might contribute useful material for critical analysis in their formal journal.

In tutorials, students reflected on and discussed critical incidents that had occurred during their service experiences. They then practiced writing a critical incident report prior to the summative assessment. Students were guided in the appropriate criteria for writing these reports, which included: clarity; using a logical structure; demonstrating critical reflection and analysis; and evaluating how this would inform their future action.

The summative oral presentations concerned students' critical reflections on the enhancement of the employability skills they had gained or developed during their service and were co-assessed by the teacher (Deeley, 2014). In the content of their presentations, students were required to demonstrate their critical thinking skills, knowledge and understanding. In the delivery of the presentations, students were expected to demonstrate good communication skills. These skills were assessed in terms of verbal clarity, fluency and pace. Prior to this summative assessment, students received formative feedback on their oral presentations on the nature of their placement and their role within the service agency. Although most of the students had experienced some formatively assessed oral presentations in other courses in their undergraduate studies, none of them had ever experienced summative co-assessment. Indeed, this type of assessment was unique and innovative within the university. To some extent it was rather daunting to implement such a new method of assessment and so a weak model of co-assessment (Heron, 1988) was chosen, where already established criteria were used, because this was deemed to be less risky.

In this co-assessment, students self-assessed their own oral presentation and I also assessed each presentation. The university's marking scheme for the social sciences was applied, using alphabetical grades with subsidiary numerical bands, for example, A1. Marking sheets were designed to enable each student and the teacher to tick a box next to the grade they thought was most appropriate for the presentation in terms of its content and delivery. Additionally, and vital to this process, each student and I wrote critical comments on the form to justify the marks we had given. Following the presentations, I met each student individually in a separate room to allow a private discussion of our marks. The meeting concluded when a consensus was reached which was done either through immediate agreement or following negotiation. It had previously been made clear verbally and in the course documentation that should an agreement not be reached, I would retain the authority to decide the final mark. The agreed mark contributed 10% to the course grade overall, which in turn, would account for 2.5% of a student's final degree classification. To ensure reliability and validity, students' written summaries of their oral presentation were available for scrutiny by the external examiner.

Methods

The aims of the research were firstly, to examine the effects of the non-traditional forms of assessment used in this course on the students' perceptions and awareness of their learning. In particular, there was a focus on the effects of critical reflection. Secondly, the project aimed to examine the effectiveness of employability skills assessment through oral presentations (Deeley, 2014). To achieve these aims, the objectives were to investigate students' perceptions of the impact on their learning of: critical reflection on service experiences that were related to academic theory; journal writing; and the dissemination of 'critical incidents' within tutorials. Further objectives were to investigate: the development of students' employability skills; efficacy of oral presentations and students' self-assessments; and the effective negotiation and agreement of appropriate marks.

The study was conducted during the period it was being taught in the session of 2011. To achieve the aims of the research, this project was qualitative in design, with eight individual semi-structured interviews held with the students. At the end of the course and after all the individual interviews had been conducted, a focus group with all the students together was held. The aim of the focus group was to generate a clear understanding of the group's view of their learning through their critical reflections and the non-traditional assessment methods. Ultimately, this approach served to validate and clarify the data analysis. As this was a small class, further written data from service-learning students' coursework was collected in 2013 after ethical approval had been obtained.

Participants

As there were only eight students on the course in 2011, it was imperative that care was taken to ensure their anonymity. As the class consisted of four men and four women, it was deemed appropriate that all references to them be feminised in order to ensure anonymity. For consistency, further data collected from the later cohort of twenty students in 2013 were also feminised.

Ethics

Assurance of anonymity was made to the students in the plain language statements which gave them information about the research study, and verbally at the start of the individual interviews. As this was practitioner research where I had a double role as the researcher and also the teacher of the course, it was imperative that the students were assured that their participation or non-participation would not affect the outcome of their studies, assessment, or degree. Students were also assured that their participation or non-participation would neither adversely nor favourably affect our student-teacher relationship. It was absolutely essential that students had a clear understanding that they were under absolutely no obligation to participate in the study. The students were also aware that they could withdraw at any time from the study and without giving any reason. The integrity of the coursework grades was maintained because the assignments were all marked anonymously, second marked by another teacher and examples of their coursework were later scrutinised by an external examiner. Approval for the study was given by the university's ethics committee and written informed consent was obtained from all the students before the research commenced.

Although the participants were assured that the student-teacher relationship would not be adversely affected, it is possible that positive responses were induced through 'the so-called "halo" or "Hawthorne" effect' (Silverman, 2001, p. 233). It must also be noted that this was a small scale study so that its findings are not claimed to be representative of all service-learning courses.

Data collection

The individual interviews and focus group each lasted between 30 and 50 minutes. Using open-ended questions and a semi-structured approach to the interviews and focus group, allowed the students to talk freely about their views on the non-traditional assessment methods of the course. They also spoke of the merits and challenges of critical reflection. The students were asked about their early expectations of the course and what had influenced them to enrol on the course. They were also asked how the use of critical reflection in the formative and summative assessment had impacted on their learning. The oral presentations were also discussed, particularly in terms of what the students felt about negotiating and agreeing marks with me, as the teacher.

All the students agreed to the digital recording of the interviews and focus group. The recordings were transcribed verbatim and the students' written summaries of their oral presentations were also used as data. As referred to earlier, an additional data set was used that consisted of written coursework from the 20 students who were engaged in the subsequent service-learning course in 2013.

Data analysis

All the data from the interviews were scrutinised carefully by initially reading the transcripts and then by reading them again while at the same time listening to the recorded interviews. A further close reading of the transcripts allowed clear and overarching themes, arising from the data, to be identified. Subsequently, several concept maps were drawn to reflect these emerging themes (Hay and Kinchin, 2006). This concept mapping was further refined in order to clarify and confirm the thematic framework. Following this, intensive micro-analysis of each transcript and concept maps was undertaken. This produced relevant connections between themes which could be supported by evidence embedded in the data.

Findings

The effects on students confronting non-traditional assessment methods within an unconventional approach to learning was an area of investigation that promised to bear rich fruits of new understanding. It was hoped that this understanding would provide insight to students' perceptions and gather evidence to inform and instigate further innovations in learning and teaching. Service-learning requires students to be active learners. This research gave students an opportunity to voice their opinions about how they learned through assessment and what effects it had on them. This is useful for future teaching and research in service-learning and is also transferable to courses within a more traditional pedagogical framework.

Expectations

Each student was asked to reflect on why they had chosen the service-learning course and whether its type of assessment had influenced their choice. What was overwhelmingly apparent from the students' responses was that they all believed that service-learning was unique and different from what they had experienced so far in their undergraduate studies. Some of them said they were bored with the 'exact same format' of essays and exams found in traditional courses every year, and for which they felt they were 'jumping through hoops'. Service-learning appealed to them as interesting because it was something different to do, with one student admitting to being 'actually quite excited about' because it was a 'different challenge'. Despite some of the students not being sure or confident about what the course entailed initially, 'it all fell into place' soon enough. Other students felt that not having an exam was 'a pull' (an attraction) either because they found exams stressful or their exam performance in the past had not been as good as they had wished.

Formative assessment

As this course was a new experience for all the students, it was important for them to understand what was involved in their assessment. They had all given oral presentations in their earlier undergraduate years of study and had engaged in formative self-assessment, however, none of the students had experience of co-assessment, nor had they experienced oral presentations as part of their summative assessment. Each student, however, gave a formatively co-assessed oral presentation early in the course to help them practice their skills.

It is important to note that this coursework would have an impact on their final degree classifications, so it should be acknowledged that these students were taking a risk in that they had no idea how they might perform at the onset of the course. It was perhaps this situation that contributed to the development of high levels of trust being evident in class between the students themselves and between the students and the teacher. To reinforce this notion, a student who had considered taking the course but ultimately decided against it explained that her decision had been strategic because she wanted 'to play it safe' and take a different course with more traditional assessment with which she was already familiar.

It was interesting to discover that the students' perceptions of formative assessment in previous classes were negative. They said that they would ask, 'Why are we doing all these formative (assessments), they don't count for anything, they're taking up my time'. In this service-learning course, however, they clearly understood that formative assessment represented an opportunity for them to learn and to improve their work. This was exemplified by a student describing the formative assessment as 'a part of the learning process' that had benefited her. Her peers reinforced this view saying, 'It has really helped me' and it is 'such a good opportunity because you can learn from it', which reflects the findings in the literature (Jessop et al., 2012). Other students explained that the formative assessment was 'really useful, otherwise you don't really understand' and that it was 'encouraging to do one (formative assessment) first'. Overall, the students found the formative assessment to be helpful in their learning, not just strategically as in terms of what to expect, but importantly, how to learn from the experience. This resonates with the literature on learning being enhanced through effective feedback (Taras, 2003). Formative assessment thus led students to feeling more confident in themselves and less anxious about their performance. One student said that she was 'definitely a lot more relaxed' about the summative assessment, having had the previous experience of 'practice' from the formative assessment.

Reflective journals

Written guidance on journal writing was given to students at the beginning of the course. This resonated with the literature on the theory of narrative writing which was discussed in class. Verbal guidance on writing journal entries was also given to the students throughout the course and an example from my own reflective journal while engaged in international service-learning was examined as a model, as referred to in Chapter 6. The aim of the journal was for students to utilise their practical experiences to gain understanding of the theoretical and conceptual elements of the coursework (in this case, focusing on citizenship) through critical reflection. As the journals contained experiential learning, it was inevitable that students would have to write in the first person singular. This was a completely different style of writing from what they had previously been used to in academic writing, and which, according to students 'went against the grain'. This factor, in addition to the unfamiliarity of the assignment, caused them much anxiety.

The 5,000-word journals contributed to 80% of the students' overall course grades. It was, as one student explained, 'bringing it all together... all the seminars, reading and practical work experience and your own thoughts and stuff together, in the one bit of work'. Indeed, as another student exclaimed, 'that's the whole point of the challenge of this course... to critically reflect (on) this whole experience'. Most of the students were apprehensive about writing their journal, expecting the task to be very difficult. Some of them said that they were 'scared' of the prospect of writing the journal, with one student even admitting that she was 'petrified' about it. One of the other students described it as 'one of the hardest pieces of coursework... in my time at university' and another claimed that this was 'a far deeper, a far more challenging experience than the standard 3,000 word essay'. Other students were more positive, saying that this was 'interesting... it's something very different, something unique which actually might help my motivation'. It was also described as 'a chance to get your own thought into a piece of writing which I thought was very appealing... bringing in the literature and tying it together... saying what you think rather than always referencing someone else's ideas'. Mirroring this, another student commented that her journal writing was unlike writing in her other courses because it was not based on a topic read from a book. She wrote, '[i]n a nutshell for me, it's a move away from the traditional rote learning. Instead of reading the books, we get to write them!' This resonates with the idea of students taking ownership of their learning and was a source of motivation as some students asserted that they were 'looking forward to writing it'.

Despite the journal being a large piece of the coursework, one student acknowledged that 'it's an ongoing assessment almost in terms of you're doing your reflective diary every week, you're doing your reading which then relates to that every week'. The benefit of this was that 'it's going to be ingrained in my brain ... (more than an exam) where you study for it and you forget everything (afterwards)'. Reinforcing this, another student claimed assuredly that journal writing is 'excellent, I mean, a really worthwhile thing'.

Critical incidents

The practice of critical reflection is essential in service-learning. It allows students to connect their academic coursework with their service to the community. This connection serves to deepen students' understanding of theory with practice. Prior to the course, most students said they had reflected but never in any particularly structured way, as a student explained, 'I hadn't realised I was doing it until it was brought to my attention (in this course)'. Others admitted that reflection 'wasn't something I'd really thought about much (before)'. The aim of the critical incident reports, therefore, was to encourage students to become more aware of and practice the process of critical reflection in a very structured manner.

Despite numerous explanations and practical examples of critical incident report writing, the concept of a critical incident proved very difficult for students to grasp. As a student said, 'I think the word "critical" throws you at first'. They tended to associate the word 'critical' as an urgent life or death situation and thus found it difficult to change their understanding of it as merely representing a turning point. Furthermore, this 'tipping point' might almost be indiscernible and possibly could be completely overlooked. One student said that she understood 'it could be something quite subtle and it's just how you react to it that kind of makes it critical'. Another described it as 'constantly going over things ... it's more like an internal conversation with yourself and going over events or circumstances that have happened'.

Before these statements were made by the students, however, a process of identifying a critical incident and understanding its nature was painstakingly undertaken. One student said that she 'was quite daunted' by this challenge and another student admitted 'I had a very hard time getting my head around them, a very hard time', although another student was 'curious' about critical incidents. For some it took 'a wee while to grasp the concept' and was perceived as 'a hurdle to get over'. Understanding, however, usually arrived as a cathartic moment rather than as a gradual awakening. A common description of when a clear understanding of critical incidents occurred with the students was the 'penny dropped' and 'it clicked'. At times these moments occurred during the tutorial discussions when a student would sometimes be able to identify another student's experience as a critical incident. These were threshold moments in tutorials. Subsequently, students quickly acquired and developed a sophisticated understanding of critical incidents and 'what it meant to be critical'. It was described as 'a jump from normal ways of learning to critical reflection'. The students described themselves as being more alert and actively questioning information, rather than merely accepting it passively. Other effects from considering critical incidents were, as one student described it, 'actually thinking of what I'm doing, stopping and thinking'. Another student experienced the result as 'a wakening inside yourself about something that's happened or realising a change in yourself or a situation...or a change of outlook'. Interestingly, one student claimed that the 'real point' of a critical incident was what one did about it afterwards. Others agreed that the value of critical incidents was how it informed their 'future action', which suggests that using this method of reflection reinforces service-learning as a critical pedagogy. Writing critical incident reports also helped students to write reflectively in their journals. One student exemplified this saying, 'I then began to realise that there is a benefit to (writing critical incident reports)...a huge benefit towards your journal if you do this correctly and grasp why you're doing it'.

Oral presentations

All the students had given oral presentations prior to the course and although some of them had enjoyed this task, others remained 'nervous' about it. Nevertheless, it was regarded by all of the students that it was a useful learning experience as one of them claimed, '[I]t's an opportunity for you to express what you've learned...it's aided my learning'. It also motivated students because 'knowing that you've got to do a presentation...you learn it more, you make more of an effort'. Critical self-reflection was a vital component in the students' summative oral presentations and students thought that this was conducive to learning that they did not forget, unlike much of what they learned in traditional courses. This type of assessment was of further value in that it increased students' confidence. All the students said that they had prepared carefully for their presentation as they did not want to appear foolish in front of their peers. One student said emphatically, 'I thought (oral presentations) were really good and I think we should have more of them'. Ultimately, students were convinced of the benefits of giving oral presentations not least because they were regarded as important for developing their communication skills. Different facets of communication skills were further enhanced through the processes of co-assessment, in particular involving the discussions about and negotiation of marks.

The summative oral presentations gave students the opportunity to demonstrate their critical reflections on the skills and attributes they had developed in the course as a whole, but especially through their giving service to the community. Critical reflection was a skill used by a student, for example, while giving service in a day care centre for frail and elderly people. She had encountered a situation where two elderly people were bullying another elderly person and the student had not known immediately what to do in those circumstances. After critical reflection and discussion in the tutorial, she felt more capable of responding appropriately should a similar situation arise in the future. In another situation, an opportunity to exercise critical reflection arose for this same student when she became very upset by the news that one of the elderly service-users, with whom she had worked closely, had died.

Co-assessment

Co-assessment can empower students. It requires students to be more involved in the assessment process and gives them a level of responsibility. In the course, co-assessment caused students to focus their thinking on the self-assessment of their oral presentations and it gave them almost immediate feedback which they could match to their own written critical comments.

Students had not experienced the process of negotiation of marks prior to this course, and one student queried how this could be possible. She questioned, '[H]ow much do I argue my point here?', fearing that her argument might invite the teacher's disapproval, which in turn, she believed, might result in the lowering of her marks. She worried that defending her position would be detrimental, but after consideration she added, 'that depends on who's teaching you and whether there's a rapport there, a trust almost'. As she recalled, '[T]rust encompasses a lot of the course, just even speaking up, you're speaking about your own weaknesses at times'. A high level of trust had developed in the class. This was extremely pertinent when a critical incident occurred during the co-assessment. In one of the individual meetings for the sharing of feedback, negotiations, and agreement of marks for the oral presentations, a student revealed to the teacher that the class, in the teacher's absence, had discussed a strategy whereby they might all secure high grades. This revealed a 'dark side' of co-assessment (Deeley, 2014, p. 46). It transpired that the students had acknowledged collectively that this would be dishonest and had nobly rejected the idea of this strategy. They agreed together to make a fair and authentic contribution to their marks, which would ultimately contribute to their degree classifications. This co-assessment experience was 'too important to waste the opportunity' by cheating. They also believed that this new type of assessment was worth preserving for future students and they did not want potentially to jeopardise the future running of the course. They also felt that co-assessment was more valuable to them than self-assessment alone as it validated their personal judgements, which resonates with Boud's (1990) view on co-assessment, as noted earlier. This reinforces the ideas in the literature that collaborative work can be beneficial to students' learning (Cook-Sather et al., 2014; Bovill and Bulley, 2011; Nicol and McFarlane-Dick, 2006; Knight and Yorke, 2003).

Self-assessment

Initially, the students did not all consider themselves sufficiently proficient or confident in their self-assessment and were unsure how to rate themselves. Nevertheless, the students found the self-assessment exercise to be very useful because it entailed a considerable amount of critical self-reflection. Their self-reflection also prompted them to consider ways in which they could improve their presentations and communication skills in general. This was then reinforced by the feedback they received as part of the process of co-assessment, both for their formative and summative oral presentations.

Learning

Critical reflection was the key element in all the service-learning coursework assessment. Critical thinking and critical reflection were also the cornerstones of the seminars and tutorials in which students crucially connected theory with practice and analysed their service experiences. One student commented, '[I]t's nice just having the space to stop, think, take a step back... kind of strange that you've got to be taught that almost, it seems like common sense when you say it, but I do think you need it spelled out to you'. This affected students after the course had finished, for example, a student said that she had started 'to question things more' and another agreed saying, 'I am thinking over things a lot more than I used to'.

The students also began to be more aware of how and what they were learning and because they knew that their service experiences were unique to them as individuals, they acknowledged responsibility for their learning. With this, came the idea of 'ownership' of their learning, as referred to earlier. Rather than being passive recipients of knowledge, the students were active in making sense of their experiences, and were thus constructing their own understanding. This occurred through the combination of reading the literature, discussing theory in class and relating it to their experience, as one student said, 'I think by doing that we're learning a lot more'. They were 'reading with a purpose' and trying to 'think, well, how is that related to what we're doing?' A student explained that 'you take that idea and make it your own because you link it to something that you've done' and another said, 'it's from your perspective and it's your story'. The personalised element cemented this as deep learning, and as one student observed, '[E]xperience always lasts longer than a book'.

The students, therefore, were well engaged intellectually. The camaraderie and peer support in the tutorials imbued them with confidence and motivation. Significantly, a student enthused, '[Y]ou're wanting to come to class every week and not wanting to miss anything and see what other people are saying, what their experiences have been'. To exemplify the emerging learning community of the tutorial group, a student commented, '[Y]ou share the assumptions of the critical incidents that have happened and it really gives it so much more meaning than it would if it was just (individual)'. The benefit of sharing was further explained when '(we) really like look at it from both, like an outside perspective and your own, so that's been really good'. It also transpired that the students regularly exchanged ideas about the coursework outside class and on 'Facebook'. From the course overall, a student commented that she had 'grown a lot, a lot more independent, a lot more confident in my decisions. I think it's a great experience for me.' Another student added, 'I think a lot of people don't realise how much you can learn outside of the class really and so getting out there and being part of the community especially, you learn so much, it's incredible.'

Discussion

An essential skill that is required and developed within service-learning is critical reflection. Critical reflection is a critical thinking skill that allows students to draw together their service experiences and the academic coursework. In doing this, students create their own understanding or meaning, although it demands a high level of cognitive functioning (King, 2000). The effects of critical thinking in service-learning have been explored elsewhere (Deeley, 2010; 2007). This study reaffirms some of those effects, namely, that in stepping gingerly out of their 'comfort zone', students can find themselves in a vast space fertile with opportunities for learning. It is in this action that service-learning gives students the chance to stretch intellectually in their 'zone of proximal development' (Vygotsky, 1978, p. 86).

In order to nurture students' critical thinking skills, it is important that they have the opportunity to develop them through course assignments, whether this is within service-learning or indeed any traditional courses. From the findings of the study, it is clear that formative assessment was beneficial to the students in that they were able to recognise and understand the learning process, how they learned and what steps they could take to improve their performance. In addition to the students gaining a greater understanding of the reasons why it was of value to take part in formative assessment, it prepared them for, and made them more confident in, tackling the summative assessment. Moreover, students, in becoming more confident learners, became highly and intrinsically motivated (Boud, 1990). This led to the students' greater engagement and, subsequently, their deep learning.

It was evident that each type of assessment used in this course encouraged students' deep critical thinking skills. Participating in their own, and exposed to others', critical reflection every week of their service-learning, students built an understanding of the cognitive processes that it demands. Through their intellectual efforts, the challenges of journal writing transmuted into deep learning to the extent that their learning became 'ingrained', as one student described it. Identifying and examining critical incidents also provided opportunities for understanding the process of critical reflection and gave the students an opportunity to discover their own, and sometimes cathartic, turning points (Deeley, 2010). The students used the critical incidents to consider how they would change their thinking and behaviour in the future. Consequently, there was a potential for them to act in considered and critical ways, or what might be regarded as praxis (Freire, 1970). This reinforces the assertion that service-learning can be a critical pedagogy. The oral presentations afforded students another opportunity to critically reflect within and on their presentations as these were self-assessed as part of co-assessment. The presentations contributed to the students' high levels of motivation as they did not want 'to lose face' in front of their peers, but also because they realised that demonstrating their learning also helped them to learn further and at a deeper level. Mirroring Boud's (1990) view the students considered co-assessment more beneficial than self-assessment alone. Effective and very timely feedback was given to them on their oral presentations. Consequently, students were motivated to make great efforts to perform well. The co-assessment method used was, therefore, conducive to students' deep learning, which resonates with the literature (Knight and Yorke, 2003). It is clear that students gained confidence through the assessment, which also reflects the ideas expressed in the literature (Boud and Falchikov, 2007; Knight and Yorke, 2003; McMahon, 1999) and through the assessment, students also learned how to learn (Heron, 1988).

In many ways, the study reveals that through assessment students were enabled to learn effectively. Summative co-assessment, for example, was useful also for students' learning because intrinsically it involved feedback. This indicates that summative assessment can contribute to further learning after a course, whether it is transferable to another course of study, employment, or lifelong learning.

Students acknowledged that they had taken 'ownership' of their learning especially during co-assessment, which had also resulted in their feeling empowered (Tan, 2007; Falchikov, 2005; Taras, 2003). Overall, there is much synchronicity between this study and what is extant in the literature. What this study reveals further, however, is the less salubrious possibility within co-assessment, or its potentially 'dark side' (Deeley, 2014, p. 46). There are measures to safeguard against this, for example, with the teacher retaining the jurisdiction to determine the final mark and the requirement of the students to justify their self-assessed mark through written comments on their oral presentations. By having this safeguard, other issues of importance are also highlighted such as the validity and credibility of the assessment (Bloxham and Boyd, 2007; Knight, 2002).

From the findings of this study, it is evident that students developed intrinsic motivation through the coursework and its assessment. A light being shone on a potentially darker side of co-assessment revealed, however, that extrinsic motivation may still exist. This is perhaps inevitable as an inherent part of summative assessment. Other facets of the assessment imbued students with confidence which enhanced their learning as well as fuelling their motivation and encouraging deep learning (Falchikov, 2005; Race, 2001; Brew, 1999). These facets included formative assessment, the timeliness of feedback, especially following the oral presentations, and the validation of their self-assessment through co-assessment. It is through these aspects that deep learning was confidently assured.

Conclusion

This chapter has focused on the use of critical reflection within and on assessment. Service-learning is a non-traditional method of learning and teaching and it is asserted that in good practice, course aims and intended learning outcomes align with assessment methods. It is appropriate, therefore, that alternative and innovative methods of assessment are applied. The effects of assessment designed to encourage students' critical and reflective thinking skills on students themselves were investigated. The factors involved in this study were the coursework assignments, such as the reflective journals, critical incident reports that prepared students for thinking and writing reflectively, and the oral presentations. In addition, there were the factors involved in the assessment, such as feedback, self-assessment, and co-assessment.

A review of the relevant literature was undertaken and much of it resonated with the findings from this study. This study, however, helps to fill a gap in the service-learning research literature by demonstrating qualitative evidence of students' reflective responses on their learning. The findings were consistent with and validated by other studies undertaken with service-learning students (Deeley, 2014; 2010; 2007).

Service-learning requires critical reflection as a tool to combine the associated academic coursework with students' service to the community. When students' critical and reflective thinking skills are assessed explicitly through innovative methods that are designed for learning as well of learning, there can be huge rewards. The empirical evidence in this study reveals that students' intrinsic motivation is germinated, their confidence is built, and they are empowered by taking responsibility for their own learning, firstly, through making sense of their experiential learning and, secondly, through summative co-assessment. Subsequently, students experience deep learning, which is transferable and contributes to their lifelong learning. There are risks involved, however, in approaching learning and teaching outside conventional and well trodden paths, as discovered in this study. There may also be fear associated with this less traditional, collaborative approach (Stefani, 1994). The rewards, however, are clearly evident for students. The rewards and other effects on university teachers, however, remain an area ripe for investigation.

Vital to the nurturing of critical thinking is its purpose. It is clear that students can become more critically aware through the processes of service-learning and its assessment. This can lead to critical action or praxis and thus ultimately to critical being (Barnett, 1997). With a focus on criticality, this reiterates my assertion that service-learning can be perceived as a critical pedagogy, which ultimately may lead to students' critical action and social change.

8
Conclusion

Overview

Throughout this book I have sought to encapsulate and critically analyse different theoretical and practical aspects of service-
learning. In one sense, the structure of the book mirrors that of
service-learning because it combines theory and practice: the first
part of the text is mainly theoretical and the second part focuses
more on practice. Throughout the book I have provided supportive
evidence from various bodies of literature. This not only strengthens
the critical perspectives taken of service-learning in higher education, but also demonstrates its broad relevance within a multidisciplinary context. Perhaps adaptability is one of the attributes that
gives service-learning broad appeal and contributes to its durability.
Of course, adaptability can be a 'double-edged sword', cutting off the
defining features of service-learning if this pedagogy is too loosely
interpreted. With a list of definitions of service-learning reaching
over two hundred (Furco, 2003), it is important that service-learning
has a theoretically rigorous grounding so that its essential meaning
is not diluted or obfuscated in the vast diversity of practice under
its name. It is also vital to the integrity of service-learning pedagogy that critical perspectives of its theory and practice are encouraged and developed through robust methodological and substantive
research.

The idea for this book was born out of my own academic need
for directly relevant and supportive material to inform my teaching
with a deeper and more critical understanding of service-learning

and to use this material with my service-learning students. Providing an in-depth theoretical analysis of service-learning may also help to inform the academic practice of other university teachers and to enhance the critical perspectives of the service-learning students in their classes. To help students learn how they learn and to become more acutely aware of what service-learning entails have also been vigorous motivating factors. The chapters in this book, therefore, can be used singularly to inform individual classes. To channel the overall flow of the book, however, cross-references have been made throughout. An overview of the broad aims of the book was set out at the beginning in Chapter 1. Consistent with these aims, in conclusion it can be summarised briefly that:

- service-learning was defined and outlined, with its potential functions and outcomes, in Chapter 2;
- a theoretical model for this type of learning was explored in Chapters 3 and 4; the practice and effects of critical reflection as part of service-learning was examined in Chapter 5;
- examples of academic writing in service-learning through students' coursework and model examples provided from my experience were demonstrated in Chapter 6; and
- students' perspectives of using critical reflection within and on assessment were investigated in Chapter 7, which were grounded in empirical evidence from my own practitioner research.

The purpose of this final chapter then is to draw together the various threads of the book into the fabric of a summary analysis. This necessitates revisiting briefly the main points in each of the chapters. A critical evaluation is then made with a number of observations and recommendations for future service-learning research. The final part concludes with a few of my critical reflections.

Summary analysis

Service-learning is a modestly simple label for what might be considered a very powerful pedagogy that can intrinsically motivate students to think critically, develop deep and lifelong learning, and spur them to critical action on a personal level for individual development and on cultural and structural levels for social justice.

Service-learning is a metaphorical key that can unlock a gateway that leads to: opportunities for developing a vast array of skills and attributes; alternative, exciting, and progressive ways of learning and teaching; further insight to, and raised awareness of, societal problems and issues; and not least, to active and civic engagement. Service-learning is quite simply service to others and student learning. Ideally, these two factors are balanced through mutual benefit and reciprocity. This resonates with a Communitarian perspective where, in a 'good society', there is a balance between the individual and the 'common good'.

This function of Chapter 1 was to provide a general introduction by presenting and outlining the overall aims of the book. The organisational structure of its contents was then mapped for easy navigation. Chapter 2 began by exploring service-learning from a historical perspective in order to contextualise it within education. The concepts of citizenship, citizenship education, and civic engagement are all relevant to service-learning. Indeed, service-learning may be regarded as a form of citizenship education. Subsequently, the chapter sought to explore various interpretations of service-learning in order to distil a consensus of meaning through an examination of the plethora of definitions, principles, and characteristics evident in the literature. In conclusion of the substantive body of this chapter, a vista was presented of some of the potential outcomes of service-learning. Some of these outcomes were drawn from my own research (Deeley, 2007), as well as from other service-learning literature. To begin to understand how these outcomes might arise, it is of value, indeed necessary, to perceive a theoretical framework for service-learning. Claiming that the idea of service-learning originates from Dewey is, in a sense, accurate, although he did not actually refer to service-learning per se. Merely citing Dewey, however, does not produce a critical explanation as to why service-learning can be an effective pedagogy. The gnawing question of 'why it works' led me along several research paths and to Chapter 3. Before moving on to investigate this, however, it is perspicacious to note that the question 'why it works' is counterbalanced by the critical question of, 'why it does not work'. It appears that these two questions may belong to 'two sides of the same coin', in other words, what accounts for the success of service-learning, ironically, can also account for its failure to be effective with some students. It is important to consider both positive and negative aspects of service-learning if a critical perspective is to be taken. This was referred to in Chapter 2 (Deeley, 2014, 2010; Jones et al., 2005; Jones, 2002) and is critically evaluated further here.

Nevertheless, the chronic perplexity of how and why service-learning 'works' continued to vex me. Studying educational literature opened several conceptual doors into various learning theories and perspectives which uncannily resonated with my knowledge of service-learning. I found that I could identify certain aspects of theory that were glaringly evident within service-learning. This discovery was exciting and enthused me on a quest to find a potentially satisfactory solution to the unresolved puzzle of the reasons why service-learning is such a powerful pedagogy. I found that by deconstructing the elements that constitute service-learning, a theoretical paradigm could be drawn, which could account for its effectiveness while at the same time, providing it with a rigorous framework. Chapter 3 attempts to encapsulate the essence of this in building a theoretical foundation, while Chapter 4 extends this construction by adding further scaffolding to the mansion of service-learning, in the form of critical theory and critical pedagogy.

This book is concerned with service-learning in higher education so it involves looking at how we understand the world and construct meaning of our experiences as adults. This does not mean to say, however, that we should discount our early learning because this is relevant to a theoretical paradigm for service-learning. Chapter 3 takes into account the notions and processes of thinking and language which are importantly connected. This has relevance, too, for students in terms of dialogue within reflective tutorials and academic writing that is expressed through the narrative and personal storytelling within their reflective journals. It was asserted in Chapter 3 that we construct our world and our understanding of it. This infers that our understanding is not irrefutable and, consequently, is subject to change. The key to unlocking opportunities for change is critical reflection in the process of an experiential learning cycle. It is here particularly that service-learning draws heavily on Dewey's philosophy of education and ideas of progressive and experiential learning that contribute to a harmonious and democratic society. Another contribution to this paradigm is collaborative learning as it represents a more democratic approach to learning and teaching. This also demands change in the teacher's role and position within the service-learning classroom. Thinking about adult learning in conjunction with critical reflection and experience leads to considering the effects of change, both on a personal level for students and on a cultural and structural level with regard to wider society. Massive change on a personal level thus brings in the notion of transformative learning theory to the mix of other theories functioning in this paradigm. Changes on a cultural and structural level, however, require students to act critically through social and political routes. This extends the paradigm to include critical theory, which enables service-learning to be perceived as a critical pedagogy, which was the focus of Chapter 4.

The major and fundamental assertion that was made in Chapter 4 concerns service-learning as a critical pedagogy. Critical theory in this chapter serves as part of the paradigm that was analysed in Chapter 3 along with further elaborations of theoretical aspects also found in the previous chapter, such as transformative learning theory. Chapter 4 explored these ideas and processes, drawing on the ideas of Freire (1970; 1972; 1985), particularly with the notion of conscientisation. References to the autobiography of Malcolm X (1968) were made to illustrate critical points that demonstrate how change can occur through raised levels of consciousness. On an empirical level, evidence from my own pedagogical research studies also demonstrates the effects of change on service-learning students from being actively engaged in critical reflection and consciousness raising. Change is a potential outcome of service-learning, and it brings with it certain ethical ramifications and responsibilities for the teacher. There are also risks associated with this, for example, potential indoctrination where students could be encouraged by the teacher to believe that certain changes in society should be made for a variety of reasons and subsequently enacted by the students. This is discussed further in the critical evaluation that follows. At the heart of this chapter lies the issue of raising awareness to enable students to develop their critical thinking skills and shed false consciousness. If this can be achieved, the outcomes are not necessarily specifically predictable, but on the basis of a critical pedagogy, it would be reasonable to suggest that students' critically informed active engagement can help to create a fairer and more socially just society. This, of course, is theoretical.

The book then moved on to a more practice based perspective, looking first at critical reflection in Chapter 5. Critical reflection is part of critical thinking and belongs firmly within higher education. At the beginning of my service-learning courses, many students have claimed that they have engaged in critical reflection in the past, but it is usually an activity performed without close scrutiny of its processes. Also, before engaging in service-learning, most students have stated that they have not engaged in structured critical reflection in an academic class. It is often with some surprise to students that critical reflection forms a central core within service-learning and that they must understand this critical thinking skill in theory as well as in practice. It is important that students are aware of their thinking. By examining the processes of critical reflection, students can develop their metacognitive skills and become aware of how they learn. Consequently, this can enhance and deepen their actual learning, to the point where students are fully and actively engaged, and feel sufficiently confident to claim ownership of their learning.

It is vital that the theoretical aspects of critical reflection are examined, so this chapter referred to different models before looking at the practical aspects and stages of critical reflection. It was suggested in this chapter that critical incidents be used in service-learning as a way of structuring students' critical reflections. These incidents are versatile and can be used as practice for writing a reflective journal and as part of summative assessment. Critical incidents can also be usefully discussed in reflective tutorials with bounteous results, for example, this exercise may help other students to grasp what is meant by a critical incident and may clarify its structured process. Another benefit of discussing critical incidents in class is that it can nurture a supportive and trusting learning environment, both between the students themselves and between the students and the teacher. This is especially pertinent if the teacher is willing to share her own critical incidents with her students. Poignantly, critical incidents can sometimes occur in the classroom so it is very helpful if they can be identified and reflected on together within the class.

The chapter then looked at the potential outcomes of critical reflection, which links it thematically to other parts of the book, in particular to the previous chapter and conscientisation. A result of critical reflection can be raised awareness, where opportunities exist for new meanings to be constructed and for praxis to occur. This is in the context and understanding of service-learning being regarded as a critical pedagogy. At least, it is possible that some kind of change in students may occur through critical reflection, even though this might involve an element of discomfort. Again, the role of the teacher is important here. There is a return to the notion that the teacher holds a position of ethical responsibility, and it is incumbent upon her to be available for student support, if and when needed. Having learned to enact the skill of structured critical reflection, it is vital for students that they also learn to detach from this activity should it threaten to become compulsive. Critical reflection is crucial to effective service-learning. The academic coursework, for example, is largely dependent on honing this transferable skill. Evidence of students' critical and reflective skills is essential in service-learning coursework and its assessment. Chapter 6 subsequently and naturally progressed to encompass and examine facets of academic writing in service-learning.

Although again focusing on the more practical elements of service-learning, Chapter 6 also included supportive evidence from relevant literature. A major part of this chapter contained the presentation of authentic examples from my students' own academic work. Ethical approval to include this material was obtained from the appropriate ethics committee in the university concerned, and informed written consent was also obtained from each of the students. Selected excerpts from the students' work have been used to provide insight to the rich diversity of their experiences and critical reflection. These excerpts also serve to demonstrate the structure of critical incidents and reflective journals.

In light of critical incidents being invariably new to my students, I give them model examples for guidance from my own service-learning experiences, from volunteering both in the United Kingdom and abroad, with the international example being presented in this book. Similarly, the example of an entry journal that I use with my students is from my international service, which is also included in this chapter. To demonstrate the structure of a reflective journal, the different entries for each stage of a 'hero's journey' (Chisholm, 2000) have been made by different individual students. As a result, this does not represent one individual's complete journey but has the advantage of revealing various stages of a metaphorical journey told by different student voices. The benefit of this strategy is that it demonstrates how service-learning experiences are unique and individual.

The chapter also involved a discussion of how writing in a critically reflective genre using critical incidents and reflective journals enhances student learning. These assignments are used for summative assessment and, as such, are products of learning. Additionally, they have further value in that they require active engagement in critical thinking and reflection and, as such, they are also part of the learning process. To add weight to the assertion that applying overt critical reflection in the written narrative within critical incidents and journals, and through the spoken word in oral presentations, as part of service-learning assessment, empirical evidence from one of my research studies was disseminated in Chapter 7. This involved investigating students' reflections within and on assessment. Again, ethical approval was obtained for this research from the appropriate ethics committee at the university concerned and written informed consent was obtained from the students.

Chapter 7 began with a review of the literature on assessment, which included self-assessment, co-assessment, and feedback on assessment. In my service-learning course, I use a summative co-assessment method for students' oral presentations. This involves my assessment of their presentations and the students' own self-assessments. In light of collaborative learning, we negotiate and agree marks for this assessment (Deeley, 2014). This is innovative practice as the agreed marks directly contribute to the students' final degree classifications. It was of keen interest to investigate and discover the students' perceptions of their involvement in this type of summative assessment as well as their views on what critical reflection had meant to them during the service-learning course. The chapter disseminated the research findings, and explained the methods of data collection and analysis. Being practitioner research, there were initial ethical concerns because of my dual role as teacher and researcher. Nonetheless, ethical approval was duly granted by the university and informed written consent was given by the students prior to the commencement of the study.

The findings presented in this chapter offer a glimpse into the students' perspectives. The students' reasons for undertaking service-learning were varied, but there is no doubt that the unconventional course assessment methods were an attraction. It was important to the students that they could familiarise themselves with these methods by engaging in formative assessment, where their marks did not contribute to the final course grade, before their final summative assessment took place. Journal writing was generally found by the students to be challenging. Exacerbating this was its weighting (80% of the overall course grade) and volume (5,000 words). The fact that students collected data for their journal by writing about their placement experiences every week was helpful in reducing their anxiety and alleviating the burden of writing their final journal for submission because they contributed to it incrementally throughout the course. Unsurprisingly, students reported that they had encountered initial difficulties in comprehending the nature of critical incidents, before grasping their meaning and function. Overall, they claimed that writing critical incident reports was beneficial to the reflective writing process. The students felt empowered by the personal responsibilities invoked by the processes of co-assessment. This counteracted its potentially 'dark side' (Deeley, 2014, p. 47) whereby students had collectively decided against giving themselves a false mark in a bid to raise their final grade.

What is of utmost pedagogical relevance in the findings of the study is that students claimed that, through service-learning and these assessment methods involving high levels of evidence in engagement of critical thinking and reflection, they had learned at a deep level which they believed would be long lasting. Students claimed ownership of their knowledge and understanding because they had been actively involved in its construction. At the heart of this lies criticality and it is service-learning that provides the foundation for its development.

Critical evaluation

Taking a critical perspective of the summary analysis presented in the previous section, several points of discussion can be raised. There is a plethora of literature that demonstrates the values and virtues of service-learning. Indeed, within this body of literature there are subtle hints of a magical quality surrounding service-learning and its potentially powerful impact on both students and teachers. It is important, however, to maintain a grounded and critical view of its pedagogical prowess. Positioning service-learning within a theoretical paradigm, as asserted in the book, serves to counterbalance effusive claims that hold little substantive reasoning or explanation of the achievements and benefits gained by service-learning. Furthermore, it is fair and pragmatic to acknowledge that service-learning also has negative as well as positive aspects.

What helps to contribute to the success of service-learning are highly motivated students and teachers. For some students, service-learning is a natural progression from their previous volunteering activities and functions as another step in their own 'hero's journey' (Chisholm, 2000), but for others, it is merely an attractive course option. Some students, however, might not perceive it in such a positive way, particularly if service-learning is a compulsory element within a university's curriculum. Lacking choice can generate a negative effect on students' perceptions of, and performance in, any course. This is not to say that if service-learning is taken as an elective course that it will always be well received by students. Far from it. The studies by Jones (2002) and Jones et al. (2005), for example, reveal an alternative perception of service-learning which involves students' resistance to this pedagogy. For example, critical reflection is a metacognitive skill for which some students may not be prepared or at the appropriate developmental stage to embrace fully (Perry, 1999). Dark and miasmic effects could also emerge from students' potentially strategic approaches to co-assessment (Deeley, 2014).

The success of service-learning requires motivated teachers who believe in the efficacy of this pedagogical approach. It could be regarded almost as a 'labour of love' because the demands of commitment, organisation, and time are high, although the unquantifiable rewards can be hugely satisfying. Nevertheless, some teachers may prefer more traditional learning and teaching methods. It is important that teachers, like their service-learning students, engage in critical reflection in order to facilitate its use and offer guidance to their students. As with students, critical reflection can also have various effects on teachers themselves. One of these effects is that, once started, critical reflection may be difficult to stop and, paradoxically, may result in frozen inertia. Here, there is a potentially inverting symbiotic relationship between critical reflection and action, in that too much critical reflection may reduce the possibility of critical action if we become overly engrossed in thinking. Similarly, too much action can inhibit critical reflection. Service-learning does not exist in a vacuum: it involves a social interaction between the teacher and students. It would be interesting, and fill a gap in the research in this field, to investigate aspects, and possible effects, of this pedagogical approach on service-learning teachers. This is also pertinent to the issue of collaborative learning and teaching.

Collaborative learning fits neatly into the parameters of service-learning, indeed, one could argue that it is an essential factor. Reflective tutorials, for example, are vital to students' understanding of their voluntary work placements as they can begin to make sense of their experiences through discussion with their peers and the teacher. Critical incidents also are usefully discussed openly for others' supportive and constructively critical comments. The sharing and co-operative learning that is involved in the typical service-learning classroom is clearly naturally collaborative. Collaboration, however, can be enacted overtly and deliberately, as in the case of summative co-assessment referred to in Chapter 7. Interestingly, it would be possible to stretch collaboration to a point whereby the balance of power between students and teacher is strikingly altered by students taking the lead in creating the circumstances for both their service and their learning (Davis et al., 2014). Despite the teacher's role being modified in student-led service-learning, it would remain essential. Indeed, there may be more scope for the teacher to focus on other potential and more critical aspects of her role, for example, as 'dissonance-engineer' (Brookfield, 2012b, p. 217). Inherent problems with a more democratic approach to learning and teaching are the idiocratic and bureaucratic academic hurdles that must be negotiated in the approval process for introducing new courses in higher education institutions. Certainly, the nature, level, and development of collaboration in service-learning are factors ripe for further investigation and research.

There can be many different aims and intended learning outcomes of diverse service-learning courses. What binds them together, however, is the notion of change, which can refer to both personal and social change. These changes may occur naturally as a result of students' increased criticality through their experience of service-learning. What is important about developing a more critical frame of mind is that it has to be facilitated by teachers and cannot be forced or thrust upon students. How students subsequently utilise their criticality is for them to decide. They must write their own agenda. For teachers to claim that service-learning must result in social justice is, at best, vague and, at worst, risks straying into the realms of indoctrination. From any academic course, it is reasonable to expect students to develop a critical perspective. Service-learning cannot guarantee that students will engage in activism or enact their critical thinking by critical action. As undergraduates, it may be unlikely that they will be in a position to enact change while on placement. In this case, service-learning can help to prepare students, not merely for their future employment through the development of employability skills and graduate attributes (Deeley, 2014), but for their lifelong learning and development as critical human beings. In other words, service-learning may have long lasting and deep effects on students that continues throughout their life's narrative. When students have graduated and become ensconced in the world of work, they may have more opportunities to instigate and lead changes. It would be fruitful to scrutinise through further research the lifelong effects of service-learning, as useful insights can be gathered (Pusch, 2004; Quiroga, 2004; Siegal, 2004).

To progress, it is vital that we keep service-learning fresh and alive and not allow it to stagnate in pools of self-satisfaction with descriptive tales or anecdotes of how specific and individual classes are taught. Service-learning offers ideal opportunities for dynamic innovations and collaborations within learning and teaching, plus mutuality and reciprocity within communities (Deeley, 2004). Rather than focusing on attempts to 'measure' its efficacy, a locus of energy would be more usefully expended on developing and improving how it works. This could involve more effective ways of facilitating students' critical reflection, improving their reflective writing skills, or discovering alternative methods of constructively aligned assessment. One example might be the use of e-learning through an online forum, such as Mahara, as a formative method of reflective writing in preparation for the summatively assessed reflective journal. The teacher could offer individual students constructive online comments on their reflective writing and connections with the academic coursework, on a regular basis throughout a service-learning course.

Findings from service-learning research could richly inform more traditional pedagogy, such as applying collaborative assessment methods from service-learning to more traditional academic learning and teaching in higher education (Deeley, 2013). This could promote service-learning to the forefront of mainstream pedagogy from its usual status of being 'at the coo's tail' (Scottish: lagging behind).

The book has explored critical perspectives of service-learning in higher education with theoretical and academic matters as its focus. It has been only part of the service-learning story because the community also plays an essential role. Unfortunately, this vital aspect has been outside the scope of this book, and it remains a field fertile for further research investigation.

Reflection

My enduring educational philosophy leads me to a strong belief that I will only ask students to do something that I am prepared to do, or have done, myself. In the early days of my teaching, I had not engaged in service-learning, and this fact hung over me like an ill-fitting garment. When the opportunity to give service to the community in Thailand arose following a service-learning conference, I summoned the courage of my convictions and jumped at the chance. At last, I felt that I would have an insight to the experience from an international perspective. Later, when I had introduced service-learning to the mainstream curriculum at my home university, there remained a gap in my experience. To address this, I gave service to my local community by volunteering in a local hospice at the same time as my students were on placement. This allowed me to keep a working journal, reflect on, and share my experiences in class with the students. It is important to note here that the anonymity and confidentiality of those to whom the students and I gave service were of primary concern and respected at all times within our classroom discussions. There was a democratic approach to the reflective process, although I discovered that students were somewhat reluctant to ask me about my voluntary work experiences at the hospice each week. Only once did this happen spontaneously. The reason for their reluctance was unclear, perhaps it was the inherent power imbalance within the classroom and/or the nature of my voluntary work, which involved feeding terminally ill patients. On reflection, it would have been helpful if I had overtly addressed their reticence. Like the students, I felt that much of my service-learning offered me rich experience and opportunity for reflection. An added bonus for me was that I have since used my experiences to facilitate and guide students in their writing critical incidents and reflective journal writing by providing authentic models from my own experiences.

As a teacher, service-learning for me is the 'crème de la crème' (Spark, 1965, p. 14) of my work in the classroom. I endeavour to be a reflective practitioner in all of my teaching, but it is during my service-learning courses especially that I am drawn to being more critically reflective. It seems that without exception, service-learning provides me with opportunities, indeed sometimes forces me, to confront or reflect on issues quite unexpectedly. Perhaps it is by my explaining the reflective process to students that renews and heightens my own critical reflections. This mirrors the idea that service-learning involves mutuality and reciprocity in the class as well as in the community. Added to this is the notion that '[c]ommitment to teaching well is a commitment to service' (hooks, 2003, p. 83). I endeavour to teach with compassion and loving-kindness. Service-learning enables and encourages me to do just that. For this reason, I hope that this book contributes to a deeper and further understanding of the architecture and elegance of service-learning.

References

Abbs, P. (1974) *Autobiography in Education* London: Heinemann.

Adorno, T. (2001) *The Culture Industry* Abingdon: Routledge.

Alerby, E., and Elídóttir, J. (2003) 'The Sounds of Silence: Some Remarks on the Value of Silence in the Process of Reflection in Relation to Teaching and Learning', *Reflective Practice* 4(1): 41–51.

Allard, C.C., Goldblatt, P.F., Kemball, J.I., Kendrick, S.A., Millen, K.J., and Smith, D.M. (2007) 'Becoming a Reflective Community of Practice', *Reflective Practice* 8(3): 299–314.

Anderson, J. (1998) *Service-Learning and Teacher Education* Washington, DC: ERIC Clearinghouse on Teaching and Teacher Education, http://chiron.valdosta.edu/whuitt/files/service2.html (accessed 16 November 2005).

Anderson, J.L. (2005) 'Community Service as Learning', *New Directions for Higher Education* 131(Fall): 37–48.

Andrade, H., and Du, Y. (2007) 'Student Responses to Criteria-Referenced Self-Assessment', *Assessment & Evaluation in Higher Education* 32(2): 159–181.

Annette, J. (2000a) 'Citizenship Studies, Community Service Learning and Higher Education', in Gardner, R., Cairns, J., and Lawton, D. (eds) *Education for Values: Moral, Ethics and Citizenship in Contemporary Teaching* London: Kogan Page, pp. 109–123.

——. (2000b) 'Education for Citizenship, Civic Participation and Experiential and Service Learning in the Community', in Lawton, D., Cairns, J., and Gardner, R. (eds) *Education for Citizenship* London: Continuum, pp. 77–92.

Arcand, I., Durand-Bush, N., and Miall, J. (2007) '"You Have to Let Go to Hold on": A Rock Climber's Reflective Process through Resonance', *Reflective Practice* 8(1): 17–29.

Aronowitz, S. (1977) 'Mass Culture and the Eclipse of Reason: The Implications for Pedagogy', *College English* 38(8): 768–774.

Ash, S.L., Clayton, P.H., and Moses (2009) *Learning through Critical Reflection: A Tutorial for Service-Learning Students (Instructor Version)* Raleigh, NC.

Astin, A.W., Vogelgesang, L.J., Ikeda, E.K., and Yee, J.A. (2000) *How Service Learning Affects Students* Executive Summary, University of California: Higher Education Research Institute.

Bannister, D., and Fransella, F. (1971) *Inquiring Man. The Theory of Personal Constructs* Harmondsworth: Penguin.

Barnett, R. (1997) *Higher Education. A Critical Business* Buckingham: SRHE/Open University Press.

Batchelder, T.H., and Root, S. (1994) 'Effects of an Undergraduate Program to Integrate Academic Learning and Service: Cognitive, Prosocial Cognitive, and Identity Outcomes', *Journal of Adolescence* 17: 341–355.

Baxter, Magolda, M.B. (ed.) (2000) *Teaching to Promote Intellectual and Personal Maturity* San Francisco, CA: Jossey-Bass.

BBC News http://www.bbc.co.uk (accessed 13 October 2012).

Beard, C., and Wilson, J.P. (2002) *The Power of Experiential Learning* London: Kogan Page.

———. (2006) *Experiential Learning* London: Kogan Page; Second Edition.

Belenky, M.F., Clinchy, B.M., Goldberger, N.R., and Tarule, J.M. (eds) (1997) *Women's Ways of Knowing* New York: Basic Books.

Belenky, M.F., and Stanton, A.V. (2000) 'Inequality, Development, and Connected Knowing', in Mezirow, J., and Associates (eds) *Learning as Transformation* San Francisco, CA: Jossey-Bass, pp. 71–102.

Berger, P.L., and Luckmann, T. (1967) *The Social Construction of Reality* London: Penguin.

Biggs, J. (2003) *Teaching for Quality Learning at University* Buckingham: SRHE/Open University Press; Second Edition.

Biggs, J., and Tang, C. (2011) *Teaching for Quality Learning at University* Maidenhead: Open University Press/McGraw-Hill Education; Fourth Edition.

Billig, S.H. (2000) 'Research on K-12 School-Based Service-Learning', *Phi Delta Kappan* (May): 658–664.

———. (2001) 'Adoption, Implementation, and Sustainability of K-12 Service-Learning', in Furco, A., and Billig, S.H. (eds) *Service-Learning. The Essence of the Pedagogy* Greenwich, CT: Information Age Publishing, pp. 245–267.

Billig, S.H., and Eyler, J. (eds) (2003) *Deconstructing Service Learning: Research Exploring Context, Participation, and Impacts* Greenwich, CT: Information Age Publishing.

Billig, S.H., and Welch, M. (2004) 'Service-Learning as Civically Engaged Scholarship', in Welch, M. and Billig, S.H. (eds) *New Perspectives in Service Learning* Greenwich, CT: Information Age Publishing, pp. 221–241.

Blackburn, J. (2000) 'Understanding Paulo Freire: Reflections on the Origins, Concepts and Possible Pitfalls of his Educational Approach', *Community Development Journal* 35(1): 3–15.

Bligh, D.A. (1972) *What's the Use of Lectures?* Harmondsworth: Penguin.

Bloxham, S., and Boyd, P. (2007) *Developing Effective Assessment in Higher Education* Maidenhead: Open University Press/McGraw-Hill Education.

Bottomore, T. (1971) 'Class Structure and Social Consciousness', in Mészáros, I. (ed.) *Aspects of History and Class Consciousness* London: Routledge & Kegan Paul, pp. 49–64.

Boud, D. (1990) 'Assessment and the Promotion of Academic Values', *Studies in Higher Education* 15(1): 101–111.

———. (2001) 'Using Reflective Writing to Enhance Reflective Practice', *New Directions for Adult and Continuing Education* 90(Summer): 9–17.

Boud, D., and Falchikov, N. (eds) (2007) *Rethinking Assessment in Higher Education* London: Routledge.

Boud, D., Keogh, R., and Walker, D. (1985) *Reflection: Turning Experience into Learning* London: Kogan Page.

Bovill, C., and Bulley, C.J. (2011) 'A Model of Active Student Participation in Curriculum Design: Exploring Desirability and Possibility', in Rust, C. *Improving Student Learning (18) Global Theories and Local Practices: Institutional, Disciplinary and Cultural Variations* Oxford: The Oxford Centre for Staff and Educational Development, pp. 176–188.

Bowen, G.A. (2005) 'Service Learning in Higher Education', in *Renaissance of Teaching and Learning* Booklet Seven Western Carolina University: Coulter Faculty Center, http://facctr.wcu/Publications/booklet_series/archive.html (accessed 21 November 2005).

Bowman, N.A., Brandenberger, J.W., Mick, C.S., and Smedley, C.T. (2010) 'Sustained Immersion Courses and Student Orientations to Equality, Justice, and Social Responsibility: The Role of Short-Term Service-Learning', *Michigan Journal of Community Service Learning* 17(1): 20–31.

Boyd, R.D., and Myers, J.G. (1988) 'Transformative Education', *International Journal of Lifelong Education* 7(4): 261–284.

Brew, A. (1999) 'Towards Autonomous Assessment; Using Self-Assessment and Peer Assessment', in Brown, S. and Glaser, A. (eds) *Assessment Matters in Higher Education* Buckingham: SRHE/Open University Press, pp. 159–171.

Bringle, R.G., and Clayton, P.H. (2012) 'Civic Education through Service-Learning: What, How, and Why?', in McIrath, L., Lyons, A., and Munck, R. (eds) *Higher Education and Civic Engagement* New York: Palgrave Macmillan pp. 101–124.

Bringle, R.G., and Hatcher, J.A. (1996) 'Implementing Service Learning in Higher Education', *Journal of Higher Education* 67(2): 221–239.

——. (1999) 'Reflection in Service Learning: Making Meaning of Experience', *Educational Horizons* 77(4): 179–185.

Brockbank, A., and McGill, I. (1998) *Facilitating Reflective Learning in Higher Education* Buckingham: SRHE/Open University Press.

——. (2007) *Facilitating Reflective Learning in Higher Education* Maidenhead: Open University Press; Second Edition.

Brookfield, S.D. (1987) *Developing Critical Thinkers* Milton Keynes: Open University Press.

——. (1990) 'Using Critical Incidents to Explore Learners' Assumptions', in Mezirow, J., and Associates (eds) *Fostering Critical Reflection in Adulthood* San Francisco, CA: Jossey-Bass, pp. 177–193.

——. (1998) 'Understanding and Facilitating Moral Learning in Adults', *Journal of Moral Education* 27(3): 283–301.

——. (2000) 'Transformative Learning as Ideology Critique', in Mezirow, J., and Associates (eds) *Learning as Transformation* San Francisco, CA: Jossey-Bass, pp. 125–148.

——. (2012a) *Teaching for Critical Thinking* San Francisco, CA: Jossey-Bass.

——. (2012b) 'On Being Taught', in Jarvis, P. (ed.) *The Routledge International Handbook of Lifelong Learning* London: Routledge, pp. 214–222.

——. (2013) *Powerful Techniques for Teaching in Lifelong Learning* Maidenhead: Open University Press/McGraw-Hill Education.

Bruster, B.G., and Peterson, B.R. (2013) 'Using Critical Incidents in Teaching to Promote Reflective Practice', *Reflective Practice* 14(2): 170–182.

Bulpitt, H., and Martin, P.J. (2005) 'Learning about Reflection from the Student', *Active Learning in Higher Education* 6(3): 207–217.

Burr, V. (1995) *An Introduction to Social Constructionism* London: Routledge.

Butin, D.W. (2003) 'Of What Use Is it? Multiple Conceptualizations of Service-Learning within Education', *Teachers College Record* 105(9): 1674–1692.

——. (2005) 'Preface: Disturbing Normalizations of Service-Learning', in Butin, D.W. (ed.) *Service-Learning in Higher Education. Critical Issues and Directions* Basingstoke: Palgrave Macmillan, pp. vii–xx.

——. (2010) *Service-Learning in Theory and Practice* Basingstoke: Palgrave Macmillan.

Campbell, J. (1993) *The Hero with a Thousand Faces* London: Fontana.

Campus Compact (2013) http://www.campus.org (accessed 9 September 2013).

Caron, B., Genereux, D.P., and Huntsberger, B. (1999) *Service Matters: The Engaged Campus* Providence, RI: Campus Compact.

Carroll, L. (1993) *Alice's Adventures in Wonderland* and *Through the Looking-Glass* Hertfordshire: Wordsworth Editions Limited.

CBI (2009) *Future Fit. Preparing Graduates for the World of Work* London: CBI.

Chadwick, A., and Heffernan, R. (eds) (2003) *The New Labour Reader* Cambridge: Polity Press.

Chisholm, L.A. (2000) *Charting a Hero's Journey* New York: International Partnership for Service-Learning.

Cipolle, S.B. (2010) *Service-Learning and Social Justice* Lanham, MD: Rowman & Littlefield, Inc.

Clayton, P.H., Bringle, R.G., Senor, B., Huq, J., and Morrison, M. (2010) 'Differentiating and Assessing Relationships in Service-Learning and Civic Engagement: Exploitative, Transactional, or Transformational', *Michigan Journal of Community Service Learning* (Spring) : 5–22.

Cmnd Paper (1942) *Social Insurance and Allied Services* London: HMSO.

Cole, M., John-Steiner, V., Scribner, S., and Souberne, E. (eds) (1978) *Vygotsky, L.S. Mind in Society. The Development of Higher Psychological Processes* Cambridge, MA: Harvard University Press.

Congreve, W. (1971) *The Way of the World* London: Ernest Benn Limited.

Cook-Sather, A., Bovill, C., and Felten, P. (2014) *Engaging Students as Partners in Learning and Teaching* San Francisco, CA: Jossey-Bass.

Cooks, L., and Scharrer, E. (2006) 'Assessing Learning in the Community Service Learning: A Social Approach', *Michigan Journal of Community Service Learning* (Fall): 44–55.

Cranton, P. (1994) *Understanding and Promoting Transformational Learning* San Francisco, CA: Jossey-Bass.

——. (2002) 'Teaching for Transformation', *New Directions for Adult and Continuing Education* 93(Spring): 63–71.

——. (2006) *Understanding and Promoting Transformative Learning* San Francisco, CA: Jossey-Bass; Second Edition.

Creme, P. (2005) 'Should Student Learning Journals be Assessed?' *Assessment & Evaluation in Higher Education* 30(3): 287–296.

Daigre, E. (2000) 'Toward a Critical Service-Learning Pedagogy: A Freirean Approach to Civic Literacy', *Academic Exchange* (Winter): 6–14.

Davis, A. (1988) in Yancy, G. (ed.) *African-American Philosophers* New York: Routledge.

Davis, C., Coombs, O., Darragh, U., O'Connor, B., and O'Donnell, F. (2014) 'Should Student Led Service Learning Be an Integral Part of the University?', Glasgow: Presentation at the 7th Annual University of Glasgow Learning and Teaching Conference, 10 April 2014.

Dawson, J. (2003) 'Reflectivity, Creativity, and the Space for Silence', *Reflective Practice* 4(1): 33–39.

Deeley, S.J. (2004) 'The Impact of Experience', in Tonkin, H. (ed.) *Service-Learning across Cultures* New York: International Partnership for Service-Learning and Leadership, pp. 197–232.

——. (2007) 'Understanding the Effects of Service-Learning on Students in Higher Education', University of Glasgow: unpublished dissertation for MEd (Academic Practice).

——.(2010) 'Service-Learning: Thinking Outside the Box', *Active Learning in Higher Education* 11(1): 43–53, http://alh.sagepub.com/content/11/1/43.

——. (2013) *Co-Assessment and Service-Learning.* Unpublished presentation paper: 4th Asia-Pacific Conference on Service-Learning, Lingnan University, Hong Kong, 4–7 June, 2013.

——. (2014) 'Summative Co-assessment: A Deep Learning Approach to Enhancing Employability Skills and Attributes', *Active Learning in Higher Education* 15(1): 39–51, http://alh.sagepub.com/content/15/1/39.

Dewey, J. (1916) *Democracy and Education* New York: Macmillan.

——. (1927) *The Public and Its Problems* Chicago, IL: Swallow Press, Inc.

——. (1933) *How We Think* New York: Houghton Mefflin Company.

——. (1938) *Experience and Education* London: Macmillan.

Dickens, C. (1854) *Hard Times* London: Nelson and Sons Ltd.

Dimitrov, G., and Boyadjieva, P. (2009) 'Citizenship Education as an Instrument for Strengthening the State's Supremacy: An Apparent Paradox?', *Citizenship Studies* 13(2): 153–169.

Dochy, F., Segers, M., and Sluijsmans, D. (1999) 'The Use of Self-, Peer and Co-assessment in Higher Education: A Review', *Studies in Higher Education* 24(3): 331–350.

Donnison, D. (1991) *A Radical Agenda: After the New Right and the Old Left* London: Rivers Oram Press.

Dreuth, L., and Dreuth-Fewell, M. (2002) 'A Model of Student Learning in Community Service Field Placements', *Active Learning in Higher Education* 3(3): 251–264.

Driscoll, A., Holland, B., Gelmon, S., and Kerrigan, S. (1996) 'An Assessment Model for Service-Learning: Comprehensive Case Studies of Impact on Faculty, Students, Community, and Institution', *Michigan Journal of Community Service Learning* 66–71.

Education for Citizenship in Scotland (2002) http://educationscotland.gov. uk/images/ecsp_tcm4–122094.pdf (accessed 3 June 2014).

Elliott-Kemp, J., and Rogers, C. (1982) *The Effective Teacher: A Person-Centred Development Guide* Sheffield: Pavic Publications.

English, L.M. (2001) 'Ethical Concerns Relating to Journal Writing', *New Directions for Adult and Continuing Education* 90(Summer): 27–35.

Enos, S., and Troppe, M. (1996) 'Curricular Models for Service Learning', *Metropolitan Universities: An International Forum: Service Learning* 7(1): 71–84.

Eyler, J.S. (2000) 'What Do We Most Need to Know About the Impact of Service-Learning on Student Learning?', *Michigan Journal of Community Service Learning* 7: 11–17.

Falchikov, N. (2005) *Improving Assessment through Student Involvement. Practical Solutions for Aiding Learning in Higher and Further Education* London: RoutledgeFalmer.

Fitzpatrick, T. (2005) *New Theories of Welfare* Basingstoke: Palgrave Macmillan.

Flanagan, J.C. (1954) 'The Critical Incident Technique', *Psychological Bulletin* 51(4): 327–358.

Fook, J., and Gardner, F. (2007) *Practising Critical Reflection* Maidenhead: Open University Press/McGraw-Hill Education.

Fransella, F. (1970) '... And Then There Was One', in Bannister, D. (ed.) *Perspectives in Personal Construct Theory* London: Academic Press, pp. 63–89.

Freire, P. (1970) *Pedagogy of the Oppressed* London: Penguin.

——. (1972) *Cultural Action for Freedom* Harmondsworth: Penguin.

——. (1985) *The Politics of Education* South Hadley, MA: Bergin & Garvey.

——. (2000) *Cultural Action for Freedom* Boston: Harvard Educational Series.

Fromm, E. (1968) *The Revolution of Hope* New York: Harper & Row.

——. (1978) *To Have or to Be?* London: Jonathan Cape.

Furco, A. (2003) 'Issues of Definition and Program Diversity in the Study of Service-Learning', in Billig S.H. and Waterman, A.S. (eds) *Studying Service-Learning* Mahwah, NJ: Lawrence Erlbaum Associates, Inc., Publishers, pp. 13–33.

Gelter, H. (2003) 'Why Is Reflective Thinking Uncommon?', *Reflective Practice* 4(3): 337–344.

Gifford, C. (2004) 'National and Post-national Dimensions of Citizenship Education in the UK', *Citizenship Studies* 8(2): 145–158.

Giles, D.E., and Eyler, J. (1994a) 'The Impact of a College Community Service Laboratory on Students' Personal, Social, and Cognitive Outcomes', *Journal of Adolescence* 17(4): 327–339.

——. (1994b) 'The Theoretical Roots of Service-Learning in John Dewey', *Michigan Journal of Community Service Learning* 1(1): 77–85.

——. (1998) 'A Service Learning Research Agenda for the Next Five Years', *New Directions for Teaching and Learning* 73(Spring): 65–72.

Gill, S. (2014) 'Mapping the Field of Critical Narrative', in Goodson, I. and Gill, S. (eds) *Critical Narrative as Pedagogy* London: Bloomsbury Academic, pp. 13–37.

Grabove, V. (1997) 'The Many Facets of Transformative Learning Theory and Practice', *New Directions for Adult and Continuing Education* 74(Summer): 89–96.

Gramsci, A. (1971) *Selections from the Prison Notebooks* London: Lawrence and Wishart.

Gray, D. (2001) *A Briefing on Work-Based Learning* York: LTSN Generic Centre, Assessment Series No.11.

Greenwood, J., and Robins, L. (2002) 'Citizenship Tests and Education: Embedding a Concept', *Parliamentary Affairs* 55: 505–522.

Grenfell, M., and James, D. (1998) *Bourdieu and Education* London: Falmer Press.

Habermas, J. (1987) *Knowledge and Human Interests* Cambridge: Polity Press.

Halonen, J.S. (1995) 'Demystifying Critical Thinking', *Teaching of Psychology* 22(1): 75–81.

Hart, M.U. (1990) 'Liberation through Consciousness Raising', in Mezirow, J., and Associates (eds) *Fostering Critical Reflection in Adulthood* San Francisco, CA: Jossey-Bass, pp. 47–73.

Hart, T. (2008) 'Interiority and Education: Exploring the Neurophenomenology of Contemplation and Its Potential Role in Learning', *Journal of Transformative Education* 6: 235–250.

Harvey, L., and Knight, P.T. (1996) *Transforming Higher Education*. Buckingham: SRHE and Open University Press.

Hay, D.B., and Kinchin, I.M. (2006) 'Using Concept Maps to Reveal Conceptual Typologies', *Education & Training* 48(2/3): 127–142.

Hayes, E., and Cuban, S. (1997) 'Border Pedagogy: A Critical Framework for Service-Learning', *Michigan Journal of Community Service Learning* (Fall): 72–80.

Heidegger, M. (1968) *What Is Called Thinking?* New York: Harper & Row.

Heron, J. (1988) 'Assessment Revisited', in Boud, D. (ed.) *Developing Student Autonomy in Learning* London: Kogan Page; Second Edition, pp. 77–90.

Hettich, P. (1976) 'The Journal: An Autobiographical Approach to Learning', *Teaching of Psychology* 3(2): 60–63.

Hickson, H. (2011) 'Critical Reflection: Reflecting on Learning to Be Reflective', *Reflective Practice* 12(6): 829–839.

Hiemstra, R. (2001) 'Uses and Benefits of Journal Writing', *New Directions for Adult and Continuing Education* 90(Summer): 19–26.

Hinchliffe, G., and Jolly, A. (2011) 'Graduate Identity and Employability', *British Educational Research Journal* 37(4): 563–584.

Hirsi Ali, A. (2008) *Infidel* London: Simon & Schuster.

Hodgson, S.H. (1878) *The Philosophy of Reflection* London: Longmans, Green, and Co. Volumes I and II.

Hollander, E., and Hartley, M. (2003) 'Civic Renewal: A Powerful Framework for Advancing Service-Learning', in Jacoby, B., and Associates (eds)

Building Partnerships for Service-Learning. San Francisco, CA: Jossey-Bass, pp. 289–313.

hooks, b. (1995) *Killing Rage. Ending Racism* New York: Henry Holt and Co.

——. (2003) *Teaching Community* London: Routledge.

——. (2009) 'Confronting Class in the Classroom', in Darder, A., Baltodano, M., and Torres, R.D. (eds) *The Critical Pedagogy Reader* London: RoutledgeFalmer, pp. 135–141.

Horkheimer, M. (1995) *Critical Theory. Selected Essays* New York: Continuum.

Howard, J. (2003) 'Service-Learning Research: Foundational Issues', in Billig, S.H. and Waterman, A.S. (eds) *Studying Service-Learning* Mahwah, NJ: Lawrence Erlbaum Associates, Inc., Publishers.

Hughes, G. (2011) 'Towards a Personal Best: A Case for Introducing Ipsative Assessment in Higher Education', *Studies in Higher Education* 36(3): 353–367.

Huxley, A. (2005) *Brave New World* London: Vintage.

Illeris, K. (2003) 'Towards a Contemporary and Comprehensive Theory of Learning', *International Journal of Lifelong Education* 22(4): 396–406.

——. (2004) 'Transformative Learning in the Perspective of a Comprehensive Learning Theory', *Journal of Transformative Education* 2: 79–89.

Illich, I. (1971) *Deschooling Society* London: Calder & Boyars.

Jacoby, B. (1996) 'Service-Learning in Today's Higher Education', in Jacoby, B., and Associates (eds) *Service-Learning in Higher Education* San Francisco, CA: Jossey-Bass, pp. 3–25.

Jacoby, B., and Associates (2003) *Building Partnerships for Service-Learning* San Francisco, CA: Jossey-Bass.

Jacques, D. (2000) *Learning in Groups* London: RoutledgeFalmer; Third Edition.

Jarvis, P. (2001) 'Journal Writing in Higher Education', *New Directions for Adult and Continuing Education* 90(Summer): 79–86.

——. (2006) *Towards a Comprehensive Theory of Learning* London: Routledge.

——. (2010) *Adult Education and Lifelong Learning* London: Routledge; Fourth Edition.

——. (2012a) 'Learning to Do: Learning Practice' Glasgow: University of Glasgow seminar presentation, 11 November 2010.

——. (2012b) 'Learning from Everyday Life', in Jarvis, P. (ed.) *The Routledge International Handbook of Lifelong Learning* London: Routledge, pp. 19–30.

Jessop, T., McNab, N., and Gubby, L. (2012) 'Mind the Gap: An Analysis of How Quality Assurance Processes Influence Programme Assessment Patterns', *Active Learning in Higher Education* 13(2): 143–154.

Johnson Foundation (1989) *Wingspread Special Report* Wisconsin, U.S.A. http://teaching.colostate.edu/guides/servicelearning/principles_go (accessed 3 June 2014).

Jones, S.R. (2002) 'The Underside of Service Learning', *About Campus* (September/October): 10–15.

Jones, S., Gilbride-Brown, J., and Gasiorski, A. (2005) 'Getting inside the "Underside" of Service-Learning: Student Resistance and Possibilities', in

Butin, D.W. (ed.) *Service-Learning in Higher Education. Critical Issues and Directions* Basingstoke: Palgrave Macmillan, pp. 3–24.

Jung, C.G. (2002) *The Undiscovered Self* Abingdon: Routledge Classics.

Kearney, K.R. (2004) 'Students' Self-Assessment of Learning through Service-Learning', *American Journal of Pharmaceutical Education* 68(1): Article 29, 1–13.

Kelly, G.A. (1970) 'A Brief Introduction to Personal Construct Theory', in Bannister, D. (ed.) *Perspectives in Personal Construct Theory* London: Academic Press, pp. 1–29.

Kember, D., Jones, A., Loke, A., McKay, J., Sinclair, K., Tse, H., Webb, C., Wong, F., Wong, M., and Yeunge, E. (1999) 'Determining the Level of Reflective Thinking from Students' Written Journals Using a Coding Scheme Based on the Work of Mezirow', *International Journal of Lifelong Education* 18(1): 18–30.

Kendall, J.C., and Associates (1990) *Combining Service and Learning. A Resource Book for Community and Public Service* Raleigh, NC: NSIEE Volume 1.

Kenworthy-U'Ren, A. (2003) 'Teaching Ideas. Service Learning and Negotiation: Engaging Students in Real World Projects That Make a Difference', *Negotiation Journal* (January): 51–63.

Kerka, S. (2002) *Journal Writing as an Adult Learning Tool* Eric Digest No. 174 Columbus, OH: Eric Clearing House on Adult, Career, and Vocational Education.

King, P.M. (2000) 'Learning to Make Reflective Judgements', *New Directions for Teaching and Learning* 82: 15–26.

King, P.M., and Kitchener, K.S. (1994) *Developing Reflective Judgment* San Francisco, CA: Jossey-Bass.

Kitchener, K.S., and King, P.M. (1990) 'The Reflective Judgment Model: Transforming Assumptions about Knowing', in Mezirow, J., and Associates (eds) *Fostering Critical Reflection in Adulthood* San Francisco, CA: Jossey-Bass, pp. 159–176.

Knight, P. (2006) 'Assessing Complex Achievements', in McNay, I. (ed.) *Beyond Mass Higher Education* Maidenhead: Open University Press/SRHE and McGraw Hill Education, pp. 96–104.

Knight, P.T. (2002) 'Summative Assessment in Higher Education: Practices in Disarray' *Studies in Higher Education* 27(3): 275–286.

Knight, P.T., and Yorke, M. (2003) *Assessment, Learning and Employability* Maidenhead: SRHE and Open University Press/McGraw-Hill Education.

Knowles, M. (1968) 'Androgogy, Not Pedagogy', *Adult Leadership* 16(10): 350–386.

Kolb, D.A. (1984) *Experiential Learning: Experience as the Source of Learning and Development* Englewood Cliffs, NJ: Prentice Hall.

——. (1993) 'The Process of Experiential Learning', in Thorpe, M., Edwards, R., and Hanson, A. *Culture and Processes of Adult Learning* London: Routledge, pp. 138–156.

Kreber, C. (2004) 'An Analysis of Two Models of Reflection and Their Implications for Educational Development', *International Journal for Academic Development* 9(1): 29–49.

Labour Party Manifesto (2005) http://ucrel.lancs.ac.uk/wmatrix/tutorial/ labour%20manifesto%202005 (accessed 3 June 2014).

Lally, C.G. (2001) 'Service/Community Learning and Foreign Language Teaching Methods', *Active Learning in Higher Education* 2(1): 53–64.

Langstraat, L., and Bowdon, M. (2011) 'Service-Learning and Critical Emotion Studies: On the Perils of Empathy and the Politics of Compassion', *Michigan Journal of Community Service Learning* 17(2): 5–14.

Lawrence, D.H. (1971) *Fantasia of the Unconscious* and *Psychoanalysis and the Unconscious* Harmondsworth: Penguin.

Lisman, C.D. (1998) *Toward a Civil Society* Westport, CT: Bergin & Garvey.

Liu, G. (1995) 'Knowledge, Foundations, and Discourse: Philosophical Support for Service-Learning', *Michigan Journal of Community Service Learning* (Fall): 5–18.

Lukács, G. (1971) *History and Class Consciousness* Cambridge, MA: MIT Press.

Mabry, J.B. (1998) 'Pedagogical Variations in Service-Learning and Student Outcomes: How Time, Contact, and Reflection Matter', *Michigan Journal of Community Service Learning* (Fall): 32–47.

McFarlane, B. (2005) 'The Disengaged Academic: The Retreat from Citizenship', *Higher Education Quarterly* 59(4): 296–312.

Mackay, C. (1995) *Extraordinary Popular Delusions and the Madness of Crowds Ware* Hertfordshire: Wordsworth Editions Ltd.

Mannion, G. (2001) 'Journal Writing and Learning: Reading between the Structural, Holistic, and Post-Structural Lines', *Studies in Continuing Education* 23(1): 95–115.

Marton, F., and Säljö, R. (1984) 'Approaches to Learning', in Marton, F., Hounsell, D., and Entwistle, N. (eds) *The Experience of Learning* Edinburgh: Scottish Academic Press, pp. 36–55.

Marx, K. (1932) *Capital* Chicago, IL: Charles H. Kerr.

Marx, K., and Engels, F. (1970) *The German Ideology* Arthur, C.J. (ed.) London: Lawrence & Wishart.

Matthews, A. (2005) 'Mainstreaming Transformative Teaching', in Tripp, P. and Muzzin, L. (eds) *Teaching as Activism. Equity Meets Environmentalism* London: McGill-Queen's University Press, pp. 95–105.

McAlpine, L. (2004) 'Designing Learning as Well as Teaching', *Active Learning in Higher Education* 5(2): 119–134.

McDrury, J., and Alterio, M. (2003) *Learning through Storytelling in Higher Education* London: Kogan Page.

McEwen, M.K. (1996) 'Enhancing Student Learning and Development through Service-Learning', in Jacoby, B., and Associates (eds) *Service-Learning in Higher Education* San Francisco, CA: Jossey-Bass, pp. 53–91.

McHatton, P.A., Thomas, D., and Lehman, K. (2006) 'Lessons Learned in Service-Learning: Personnel Preparation through Community Action', *Mentoring and Tutoring* 14(1): 67–79.

McLaren, P. (2003) 'Revolutionary Pedagogy in Post-revolutionary Times: Rethinking the Political Economy of Critical Education', in Darder, A., Baltodano, M., and Torres, R.D. (eds) *The Critical Pedagogy Reader* London: RoutledgeFalmer, pp. 151–184.

McMahon, T. (1999) 'Using Negotiation in Summative Assessment to Encourage Critical Thinking', *Teaching in Higher Education* 4(4): 549–554.

Mendel-Reyes, M. (1998) 'A Pedagogy for Citizenship: Service Learning and Democratic Education', *New Directions for Teaching and Learning* 73(Spring): 31–38.

Merriam, S.B., Caffarella, R.S., and Baumgarter, L.M. (2007) *Learning in Adulthood* San Francisco, CA: Jossey-Bass.

Meyers, C. (1986) *Teaching Students to Think Critically* San Francisco, CA: Jossey-Bass.

Mezirow, J. (1978) 'Perspective Transformation', *Adult Education* 28(2): 100–110.

——. (1981) 'A Critical Theory of Adult Learning and Education', *Adult Education Quarterly* 32(1): 3–24.

——. (1990) 'How Critical Reflection Triggers Transformative Learning', in Mezirow, J., and Associates (eds) *Fostering Critical Reflection in Adulthood* San Francisco, CA: Jossey-Bass, pp. 1–20.

——. (1991) *Transformative Dimensions of Adult Learning* San Francisco, CA: Jossey-Bass.

——. (1994) 'Understanding Transformation Theory', *Adult Education Quarterly* 44(4): 222–232.

——. (1997) 'Transformative Learning: Theory to Practice', *New Directions for Adult and Continuing Education* 74(Summer) 5–12.

——. (1998) 'On Critical Reflection', *Adult Education Quarterly* 48(3): 185–198.

——. (2000) 'Learning to Think Like an Adult', in Mezirow, J., and Associates (eds) *Learning as Transformation* San Francisco, CA: Jossey-Bass, pp. 3–33.

——. (2009) 'An Overview of Transformative Learning', in Illeris, K. (ed.) *Contemporary Theories of Learning* London: Routledge, pp. 90–105.

Miller, J. (1994) 'Linking Traditional and Service Learning Courses: Outcome Evaluations Utilizing Two Pedagogically Distinct Models', *Michigan Journal of Community Service Learning* 1(1): 29–36.

Miller, K.K., Yen, S.C., and Merino, N. (2002) 'Service-Learning and Academic Outcomes in an Undergraduate Child Development Course', in Furco, A., and Billig, S.H. (eds) *Service-Learning. The Essence of the Pedagogy* Greenwich, CT: Information Age Publishing, pp. 199–213.

Mills, C. Wright (1956) *The Power Elite* Oxford: Oxford University Press.

Mintz, S.D., and Hesser, G.W. (1996) 'Principles of Good Practice in Service-Learning', in Jacoby, B., and Associates (eds) *Service-Learning in Higher Education* San Francisco, CA: Jossey-Bass, pp. 26–52.

Mitchell, T.D. (2008) 'Traditional vs. Critical Service-Learning: Engaging the Literature to Differentiate Two Models', *Michigan Journal of Community Service Learning* (Spring): 50–65.

Moely, B.E., Furco, A., and Reed, J. (2008) 'Charity and Social Change: The Impact of Individual Preferences on Service-Learning Outcomes', *Michigan Journal of Community Service Learning* (Fall): 37–48.

Moon, J. (2006) *Learning Journals* Abingdon: Routledge; Second Edition.

Nārada, M.T. (1975) *A Manual of Abhidhamma* Kandy, Sri Lanka: Buddhist Publication Society.

National Committee of Inquiry into Higher Education (1997) *Higher Education in the Learning Society* London: NICHE.

Newton, J. (2004) 'Learning to reflect: A Journey', *Reflective Practice* 5(2): 155–166.

Nicol, D.J., and McFarlane-Dick, D. (2006) 'Formative Assessment and Self-Regulated Learning: A Model and Seven Principles of Good Feedback Practice', *Studies in Higher Education* 31(2): 199–218.

OED (1979) *The Compact Edition of the Oxford English Dictionary* London: Book Club Associates.

Perry, W.G. Jr. (1999) *Forms of Ethical and Intellectual Development in the College Years* San Francisco, CA: Jossey-Bass.

Peters, R.S. (1967) *The Concept of Education* London: Routledge.

Pickford, R., and Brown, S. (2006) *Assessing Skills and Practice* London: Routledge.

Piper, B., DeYoung, M., and Lansam, G.D. (2000) 'Student Perceptions of a Service-Learning Experience', *American Journal of Pharmaceutical Education* 64: 159–165.

Porter Honnet, E., and Poulsen, S.J. (1989) *Principles of Good Practice for Combining Service and Learning. Wingspread Special Report* Racine, WI: Johnson Foundation.

Powell, J.P. (1985) 'Autobiographical Learning', in Boud, D., Keogh, R., and Walker, D. (eds) *Reflection: Turning Experience into Learning* London: Kogan Page, pp. 41–51.

Price, M., Carroll, J., O'Donovan, B., and Rust, C. (2010) 'If I was Going There I Wouldn't Start from Here: A Critical Commentary on Current Assessment Practice', *Assessment & Evaluation in Higher Education* 36(4): 479–492.

Pritchard, I.A. (2001) 'Community Service and Service-Learning in America', in Furco, A., and Billig, S.H. (eds) *Service-Learning. The Essence of the Pedagogy* Greenwich, CT: Information Age Publishing, pp. 3–21.

Pusch, M. (2004) 'A Cross-Cultural Perspective', in Tonkin, H. (ed.) *Service-Learning across Cultures: Promise and Achievement* New York: International Partnership for Service-Learning and Leadership, pp. 103–129.

Putnam, R. (2000) *Bowling Alone* New York: Simon & Schuster.

Putnam, R.D. (1995) 'Bowling Alone: America's Declining Social Capital. An Interview with Robert Putnam', *Journal of Democracy* 6(1): 65–78.

QCA Advisory Group on Citizenship (1998) *Education for Citizenship and the Teaching of Democracy in Schools* London: QCA.

Quiroga, D. (2004) 'Beyond the Comfort Zone', in Tonkin, H. (ed.) *Service-Learning across Cultures: Promise and Achievement* New York: The International Partnership for Service-Learning and Leadership, pp. 131–145.

Race, P. (2001) *A Briefing on Self, Peer and Group Assessment* York: LTSN Generic Centre.

Rainer, T. (1978) *The New Diary* Los Angeles, CA: J.P. Tarcher, Inc.

Report of the Commission on Citizenship (1990) London: HMSO.

Rhoads, R.A. (2000) 'Democratic Citizenship and Service-Learning: Advancing the Caring Self', *New Directions for Teaching and Learning* 82: 37–44.

Rocha, C.J. (2000) 'Evaluating Experiential Teaching Methods in a Policy Practice Course: The Case for Service-Learning to Increase Political Participation', *Journal of Social Work Education* 36(1): 53–63.

Rogers, C. (1961) *On Becoming a Person* London: Constable and Robinson.

——. (1969) *Freedom to Learn* Columbus, OH: Charles E. Merrill.

Rogers, C. and Freiberg, H.J. (1994) *Freedom to Learn* New York: Macmillan; Third Edition.

Rotenstreich, N. (1985) *Reflection and Action* Dordrecht: Martinus Nijhoff Publishers.

Rubin, S. (2000) 'Developing Community through Experiential Education', *New Directions for Higher Education* 109(Spring): 43–50.

Russell, T. (2005) 'Can Reflective Practice Be Taught?' *Reflective Practice* 6(2): 199–204.

Rust, C. (2007) 'Towards a Scholarship of Assessment', *Assessment & Evaluation in Higher Education* 32(2): 229–237.

Sadler, D.R. (2010) 'Beyond Feedback: Developing Student Capability in Complex Appraisal', *Assessment & Evaluation in Higher Education* 35(5): 535–550.

Samuels, M., and Betts, J. (2007) 'Crossing the Threshold from Description to Deconstruction and Reconstruction: Using Self-Assessment to Deepen Reflection', *Reflective Practice* 8(2): 269–283.

Sanghera, J. (2007) *Shame* London: Hodder & Stoughton.

Schön, D.A. (1987) *Educating the Reflective Practitioner* San Francisco, CA: Jossey-Bass.

——. (1991) *The Reflective Practitioner* Avebury: Ashgate.

Scott, N., and Seglow, J. (2007) *Altruism* Maidenhead: Open University Press/ McGraw-Hill Education.

Semino, E. (2014) 'Metaphor in End of Life Care'. Glasgow: University of Glasgow seminar presentation, 23 January 2014.

Shakespeare, W. (1967) *Romeo and Juliet* Harmondsworth: Penguin.

Shor, I. (1987) *Critical Teaching and Everyday Life* Chicago, IL: University of Chicago Press.

——. (1992) *Empowering Education. Critical Teaching for Social Change* Chicago, IL: University of Chicago Press.

Siegal, M.J. (2004) 'Making the Strange Familiar: Dealing with Ambiguity', in Tonkin, H. (ed.) *Service-Learning across Cultures: Promise and Achievement* New York: The International Partnership for Service-Learning and Leadership, pp. 147–162.

Sigmon, R.L. (1990) 'Service-Learning: Three Principles', in Kendall, J.C., and Associates (1990) *Combining Service and Learning. A Resource Book for Community and Public Service* Raleigh, NC: NSIEE Volume 1, pp. 56–64.

Silverman, D. (2001) *Interpreting Qualitative Data* London: Sage; Second Edition.

Smith, C., and Squire, F. (2007) 'Narrative Perspectives: Two Reflections from a Continuum of Experience', *Reflective Practice* 8(3): 375–386.

Southern, N.L. (2007) 'Mentoring for Transformative Learning: The Importance of Relationship in Creating Learning Communities of Care', *Journal of Transformative Education* 5(3): 329–338.

Spark, M. (1965) *The Prime of Miss Jean Brodie* Harmondsworth: Penguin.

Spring, J. (1975) *A Primer of Libertarian Education* New York: Free Life Editions.

Stanton, T.K. (1990a) 'Service Learning: Groping toward a Definition', in Kendall, J.C., and Associates (1990) *Combining Service and Learning. A Resource Book for Community and Public Service* Raleigh, NC: NSIEE Volume 1, pp. 65–67.

——. (1990b) 'Liberal Arts, Experiential Learning and Public Service: Necessary Ingredients for Socially Responsible Undergraduate Education', in Kendall, J.C., and Associates (1990) *Combining Service and Learning. A Resource Book for Community and Public Service* Raleigh, NC: NSIEE Volume 1, pp. 175–189.

Stark, E. (2007) *Coercive Control* Oxford: Oxford University Press.

Stefani, L.A.J. (1994) 'Peer, Self and Tutor Assessment: Relative Reliabilities', *Studies in Higher Education* 19(1): 69–75.

Tan, K. (2007) 'Conceptions of Self-Assessment', in Boud, D., and Falchikov, N. (eds) *Rethinking Assessment in Higher Education* London: Routledge, pp. 114–127.

Taras, M. (2003) 'To Feedback or Not to Feedback in Student Self-Assessment', *Assessment & Evaluation in Higher Education* 28(5): 549–565.

Taylor, E.W. (2001) 'Transformative Learning Theory: A Neurobiological Perspective of the Role of Emotions and Unconscious Ways of Knowing', *International Journal of Lifelong Education* 20(3): 218–236.

The Dalai Lama (2002) *An Open Heart* London: Hodder and Stoughton.

The Guardian (2008) Obituary: Michael White, June 17.

Thorpe, K. (2004) 'Reflective Learning Journals: from Concept to Practice', *Reflective Practice* 5(3): 327–343.

Tonkin, H. (1998) *Service Learning: Making Education More Meaningful Wingspread*, Wisconsin: 'International Service Learning: Constructing the World Anew' conference paper.

—— (ed.) (2004) *Service-Learning across Cultures: Promise and Achievement* New York: IPS-L.

Toole, J.C. (2001) 'Civil Society, Social Trust and the Implementation of Service-Learning', in Furco, A., and Billig, S.H. (eds) *Service-Learning. The Essence of the Pedagogy* Greenwich, CT: Information Age Publishing, pp. 53–81.

Tripp, D. (1993) *Critical Incidents in Teaching* London: Routledge.

Van Manen, J. (1977) 'Linking Ways of Knowing with Ways of Being Practical', *Curriculum Inquiry* 6: 205–208.

Vernon, A., and Ward, K. (1999) 'Campus and Community Partnerships: Assessing Impacts and Strengthening Connections', *Michigan Journal of Community Service Learning* 6: 30–37.

Vygotsky, L.S. (1962) *Thought and Language*. Edited and translated by Hanfmann, E. and Vakar, G. Cambridge, MA: MIT Press

——. (1978) *Mind in Society.* Edited by Cole, M., John-Steiner, V., Scribner, S., and Souberman, E. Cambridge, MA: Harvard University Press.

Warren, J. L. (2012) 'Does Service-Learning Increase Student Learning?: A Meta-Analysis', *Michigan Journal of Community Service Learning* 18(2): 56–61.

Weigert, K.M. (1998) 'Academic Service Learning: Its Meaning and Relevance', in *New Directions for Teaching and Learning* 73(Spring): 3–10, San Francisco, CA: Jossey-Bass.

Weil, S.W., and McGill, I. (eds) (1989) *Making Sense of Experiential Learning* Milton Keynes: SRHE and Open University Press.

Wilhelmson, L. (2002) 'On the Theory of Transformative Learning', in Bron, A., and Schemann, M. (eds) *Social Science Theories in Adult Education Research* 3 London: Transaction Publishers, pp. 180–210.

X, Malcolm with Haley, A. (1968) *The Autobiography of Malcolm X* London: Penguin.

Yorke, M. (2011) 'Summative Assessment: Dealing with the 'Measurement Fallacy', *Studies in Higher Education* 36(3): 251–273.

Index

Printed and Bound in the United States of America